# WORD, WORSHIP,
# WORLD, AND WONDER

# Word, Worship, World, and Wonder

*Reflections on Christian Living*

## Karen Lebacqz

ABINGDON PRESS
*Nashville*

WORD, WORSHIP, WORLD, AND WONDER:
REFLECTIONS ON CHRISTIAN LIVING

*Copyright © 1997 by Abingdon Press*

*This book is printed on recycled, acid-free, elemental-chlorine–free paper.*

*book design by JS. Lofbomm*

**Library of Congress Cataloging-in-Publication Data**

Lebacqz, Karen. 1945 –
    Word, worship, world, and wonder: reflections on Christian living
/ Karen Lebacqz.
        p.   cm.
    Includes bibliographical references and index.
    ISBN 0-687-02089-1
    1. Mission of the church.   2. Church.   3. Christianity—20th
century.   4. Christian ethics.   I. Title.
BV601.8.L38    1997
262'.001'7—dc21                                              97-13817
                                                                CIP

97 98 99 00 01 02 03 04 05 06—10 9 8 7 6 5 4 3 2 1

MANUFACTURED IN THE UNITED STATES OF AMERICA

*To all those hardworking pastors and laypeople*
*who have a love-hate relationship with the church,*
*and to all those who have left the institutional church*
*but still seek God's presence in their lives*

# CONTENTS

# ACKNOWLEDGMENTS

No book, however small, happens without a lot of help. I am deeply grateful to the Atlantic Seminar in Nova Scotia, and especially to Regina Coupar, for the invitation to give the lectures that formed the foundation for this book. Later audiences in Canada, notably the Winter Refresher Conference at St. Andrew's College, were remarkably insightful and helpful in suggesting readings and ideas to enlarge the project. Finally, particular thanks go to several colleagues and friends who reviewed early versions of the manuscript: Reverend Roy White; Reverend Sharon Thornton, Ph.D.; Reverend Elizabeth Thomsen, Ph.D.; and Dr. Barbara Galli. Not all of them liked it. Their criticisms large and small helped make it better. The faults that remain are my own.

# IN-BETWEEN LIVING

❧

*The Church has served a useful purpose no doubt, and we shall
honor its memory. But our pious forebears have gone and our
children have lost interest, and . . . our duty, as the remnant of this
once proud institution, is to . . . finish it up.*[1]

These challenging words set a radical agenda for the Atlantic
Seminar in Nova Scotia in 1995: Should the church exist at all?
Should we simply mourn the passing of an era, lay it to rest, and get
on with the business of living? Or is there some reason to think that
the revival of the institutional church might be important?

Mainline Protestant churches are living an in-between life—in
between a remembered time of glory, when sanctuaries were filled
to overflowing, and a possible demise. Perhaps some comfort can be
found in the words of Joseph Sittler, who queries, "Is it not possible
that the acknowledgment of an end is the precondition to the arising
of the new? . . . that the exhaustion of religious vitalities has historically been and may be again the moment for the gospel?"[2] Perhaps
the decline of the church does not signal the end of the institution
altogether but only the moment for the arising of something new.

If this is so, we are still living an in-between life—in between a
remembered time of glory, and a new shape and form and structure
that may bear little resemblance to what has gone before.[3] How do
we go about this in-between living?

This little book offers some tentative reflections on in-between
living from one who often feels herself to be in between. I think of

———11———

myself as a "sometime" Christian, with one foot in and one foot out of the church. Like many of my generation, I was active in the church as a youth and then fell away from it, getting involved in political protest movements and other organizations instead. Bonhoeffer's *Life Together*[4] challenged me to reconsider what a privilege it is to have access to the church. Those who live under political repression, those who are incarcerated (as Bonhoeffer was to be), those who are critically ill, those in non-Christian communities—to them the possibility of church would be a great gift. And so this "sometime" Christian came back to the church, slowly, painfully, hesitantly.

It has not been an altogether easy transition. Sometimes I feel that I am shut out of church; other times, I feel that God is shut out of church. Yet I have also had wonderful experiences of church— moments of revelation, times of challenge and comfort, insight and expansion that help to center me for living in this world. It is partly because of my negative experiences that I have searched for the positive images and ways of being that would bring me back to the church with bells on my toes and a song in my heart, and it is partly because of my positive experiences that I am convinced that the church can have a future. My experience of church fluctuates "in between" the negative and the positive.

In-between living is full of tension and ambiguity. I have come to think that the tensions and ambiguities of in-betweenness are what we are meant to experience. We live, after all, in between the crucifixion and the (final) resurrection. We are an in-between people, living an in-between life. We are in the wilderness—no longer in Egypt, but not yet in the promised land. We live between the "already" of Christ's coming and the "not yet" of Christ's coming again. How do we live this in-between life, and what does it mean for the church?

The role of the church, I believe, is not to be the perfect community (pace Hauerwas!), but to keep the already and the not-yet in life-producing tension. We have a vision of the shalom or righteousness that God desires; our task is to find those ways of being that will move us toward that vision. We live in the promise of fullness of life and with a proleptic vision of this promise. We have already seen God's promise fulfilled in Jesus, and yet we live in the midst of pain, injustice, and suffering. The promise is already present and still it is not fulfilled in history. The tension can be life-producing.

For me, the church will be life-producing if it keeps alive four Ws : wonder, word, worship, and world. Each is integrally related to the others. Each has its place in the work of the Body of Christ that is the church. I address each in turn, though not exactly in the order of the title. When a wise friend saw what I was doing, she said, "Oh, you should start with Wonder." So that is what I have done. Wonder is both the end point, as the title implies, and also the beginning point, as the order of chapters implies. These reflections form a circle that begins and ends in Wonder, touching Word, Worship, and World along the way. These reflections are meant to offer a small vision—one voice in an ongoing dialogue—for the possibilities of being church in an in-be-tween life.

The questions for these reflections, then, are: What does it take to live this tension in life-producing ways? How can the institutional church witness to the "already" and the "not yet" of Christian faith? How do our basic theological convictions get embodied and lived out in our worship, our incarnation, our bringing of self and gift to the altar, our going forth into the world?

I will answer these questions in a deeply personal way. My own desires, reflections, and judgments will not reflect those of all Christians, affected or disaffected. What I find life-producing might not be so for others. My reflections are biased by my social location and particular experiences as a white North American woman who was raised both in and out of the church. I speak here as a Protestant who is most familiar with "low church" polity and tradition, but who spent some time in Lutheran tradition and has taught side by side with Anglicans, Jesuits, and others from "high church" traditions. I have gained considerable respect—even envy, sometimes—for those traditions. I speak as a layperson, for although I am ordained I have never served as a parish pastor. My reflections are also informed by my study in the discipline of Christian ethics, and particularly in feminist ethics and bioethics. I shall draw on the resources of my discipline, which shapes my understanding of what is life-producing. Yet my primary purpose is to reflect not as an ethicist but as an educated layperson in the church. What do I think the renewal of the church requires? Why do I go to church? More important, why do I not go? By finding out why people go to church—and, significantly, why they stop going or never go—we can learn a lot about whether the church is fulfilling its mission in the world, and what a church might be that lives the in-between life in life-producing ways.

Finally, it is important to say that the church is preeminently God's, not ours, and certainly not mine alone. Whether the renewal of the church is important or necessary may not be in our hands. Whether the renewal of the church will bring people to God may also not be in our hands. Jesus preached the Reign of God, not the church. The Spirit moves in mysterious ways, and has the power to create the reign of God in spite of us. While I believe that the church is called to be the Body of Christ—God's body here on earth—I frankly believe that most of the time we fail miserably and that when and if we succeed it is not because of our wisdom, insight, or efforts, but because of God's grace. So it may be with the words that follow.

# WONDER

Many years ago, when I was a graduate student, one of my roommates got married. Along with her friends, fellow students, and family, she invited to the wedding the little girl who lived behind our house. This child was about four years old, and she had never been taken to church before. When we walked in the door, she beheld for the first time in her life the stained-glass windows, the rich, dark wood of the pews, the white flowers decorating the altar, the gold cross, the red carpet, the high beamed ceiling, the sheer size and beauty of it all. She stopped dead in her tracks, her little mouth formed a perfect circle, and she whispered, "Wow."[1]

It is this "wow" that the church needs, that the church wants to inspire. This is the "wow" of knowing that we stand before something impressive, mysterious, beautiful, awe-full, grand, and glorious. This is the "wow" of wonder.

In the presence of mystery, the proper response is awe or wonder. I go to church to experience wonder. If the mystery is truly present, then when we walk into a church we will be like that four-year-old child. I would like to be filled with wonder. I would like to sense the intangible yet palpable presence of God.

Yet wonder seems strangely missing from most white middle-class churches. Perhaps this is because we have been taught to emphasize the reasonable, the provable, the orderly and rational, the practical, the functional. We do not expect to speak in tongues or cry out in urgency of pain. We are embarrassed by displays of emotion in church. Although we may like the rhythm and the ritual, we want our rhythms and rituals contained. We have lost the richness of wonder. Can we get it back?

When I asked this of a clergy friend, he queried, "Is it realistic to expect a 'wow' every Sunday in church?" His caution is well taken. I remember the sense of burden I once felt when a student demanded that every single one of my classes be an inspirational experience; I am hesitant to impose that same burden on ministers who are already so often overburdened. Perhaps, however, we can at least seek moments of awe, glimpses of that which "passes understanding."[2] Perhaps, too, the burden may be lightened if we explore a bit the "wonder" that we seek to enable and ways to bring it about.

## *Wondering*

We use the term "wonder" in two distinct ways. I believe that both of these ways are important and necessary for the life of the church, for the revitalization of Word, worship, and world. Further, these ways of wondering are interconnected, and in that connection we may discover a way to overcome the seeming incompatibility between science and religion, knowledge and faith. Yet we are in danger of overemphasizing one of these ways of understanding wonder, and neglecting the other. That neglect could be fatal to the church.

The first use of "wonder" is when we are pondering something, perhaps a bit unsure or just testing out ideas or scenarios, or curious to know something. "I wonder what kind of a person she is." "I wonder how that works." "I wonder how cold it is outside today." Wonder in this sense has to do with thinking, cogitating, being interested, discovering that there is something we would like to know and trying to find out about it. The *Random House College Dictionary*[3] gives "to think or speculate curiously" as the first definition of *wonder*. This is the kind of wonder that permeates scientific discovery and intellectual endeavor of all kinds.

Wondering in this sense—being unsure, wanting to know, testing things out, pondering—is good for us. In his recent book, *An Anthropologist on Mars*, Oliver Sacks describes a scientist who had sustained frontal lobe damage and could still understand every article he read in *Scientific American* but had totally lost his ability to *care* about what he read.[4] He had lost his interest, his passion and, hence, his ability to be an excellent scientist. Intellect alone was not enough to make him a good scientist: he needed to *want* to know. He needed to wonder. Excellence in scientific endeavor, like achievement in many realms of life, appears to require an inquisitive, inquiring mind. Vitality and productivity both may depend on our ability to wonder about things.

Scientific curiosity is important, and it is not opposed to God's will for us. If the church is to be a place of wonder, the church must be a place where a thousand questions are asked and where it is all right to be like the three-year-old who always wants to know *why*. We will never know why Jesus said, "Let the little children come to me; do not stop them; for it is to such as these that the kingdom of God belongs" (Mark 10:14b). Perhaps it was because they were cute. Or because they were innocent and un-spoiled. Or simply because they wanted to be there. But perhaps it was because children are full of questions, full of curiosity, full of wonder. Perhaps—just perhaps—it was because the open and inquiring minds of children are indeed the stuff of which the kingdom of God is made. Like the three-year-old who is forever asking *why*, to approach God as a child is to approach God full of wonder: ready to search and seek and know, and ready to see mystery and stand in awe before that which we cannot know. M. Scott Peck suggests that "the path to holiness lies in questioning everything."[5] The church that wonders is the church that is alive to life and growth, alive to God.

Is this wonder threatened today? The more we stress the "bottom line" of profits, the more we run the risk of losing the kind of curiosity that is not always immediately profitable but may be enormously creative. Nonetheless, computer advertisements make clear that we still expect this kind of wonder from our children in school. We know that such wondering lies underneath much entrepreneurial endeavor and adult achievement. It fits well into our world. This kind of wonder we still have in dominant culture in America, and there is no reason not to have it also in our churches.

## *Wonderful (Wonder-full)*

There is a second sense of wonder, connected to the first and more important for the church. It is the sense of standing before something awesome, before a mystery, a majesty that we do not so much seek to know or find out about as to worship, enjoy, appreciate, absorb, soak up, and sink into with relief. "Oh, how beautiful!" "Isn't it fantastic?" "Breathtaking." These are the terms associated with wonder in the second sense, which the dictionary defines as "to be filled with admiration, amazement, or awe." This is the response of wonder of the four-year-old child entering the beautiful church for the first time. She was filled with admiration, amazement, and awe.

This wonder goes beyond the limits of scientific knowledge and curiosity. In *Mortal Lessons*, surgeon Richard Selzer describes several instances in which all his medical knowledge did not explain what was happening with his patients. He was awestruck. On one of these occasions, he discovered to his regret and chagrin that in operating on a young woman's face he had cut a tiny nerve. Her mouth was now twisted, and would always remain so. Selzer describes the scene this way:

> Her young husband is in the room. He stands on the opposite side of the bed. . . . The young woman speaks. "Will my mouth always be like this?" she asks. "Yes," I say, "it will. It is because the nerve was cut." She nods and is silent. But the young man smiles. "I like it," he says. "It's kind of cute."[6]

The young husband in this scene has offered a gesture of love that transcends and transforms the ugliness wrought by the surgeon's knife. The husband bends down to kiss his wife, to show her that their kiss still "works" in spite of the distortion of her mouth. Selzer responds by saying, "All at once I know who he is. I understand and I lower my gaze. One is not bold in an encounter with a God."

In a classic sign of humility or subservience, the surgeon lowers his gaze in recognition of the mystery, majesty, and awe of what has just transpired.[7] This is wonder in the sense of awe before human capacities that defy reason and transcend expectations, awe before love that heals in the face of death or tragedy.

Many of us have experienced this awe and mystery when friends who are dying of AIDS tell us that they are glad for the disease. Who could be glad to be struck down with AIDS at a young age, to know suddenly that all your plans, hopes, and dreams for the future are not to be? Yet many people living with life-threatening or fatal illnesses express a sense of joy because their very illness has brought them new life, new focus, a new understanding of the meaning of living and dying. It has shaken them out of the hum-drum every-dayness of life and caused their every breath to be wonder-full. They experience it as a holy antidote to everyday apathy.

In recognizing his wife's beauty despite her disfigurement, the young husband has what Joseph Sittler calls the ability not simply to *see* but to *behold*.[8] To behold something is to see in and through it the mystery of God. It is to regard it in its particularity, but to see in it an infinite preciousness. To have wonder, then, is akin to having *agape*—a kind of love that always sees others as they are, not in terms of their usefulness for us, but in terms of their place in the great scheme of God's infinite love and suffering.[9]

While some mysteries appear to call on the wonder-full in human life, others call on a mystery that transcends human capacities altogether. They defy our best abilities to explain and interpret. Selzer describes the case of "Joe," who had a large, malignant tumor on his forehead that had literally eaten away his scalp and was eating into bone tissue. Every week Selzer begged him to have surgery before it was too late: soon the tumor would eat through to the brain tissue, and Joe would die. Every week, Joe declined. Then one day Joe missed his appointment. Two weeks went by. Three. Finally Selzer went to the diner where Joe worked as a cook to get news on what had happened to him. When Selzer arrived, Joe was working behind the counter. His head had healed completely. Selzer was dumbfounded: such a large tumor does not disappear without treatment. "What happened?" he asked. "I went to Lourdes," replied Joe.[10]

The television show *Unsolved Mysteries* thrives on precisely such wonder-full stories of the mysterious. One episode told the story of a baby whose heart stopped beating at birth. A team of doctors worked for more than half an hour trying to revive the little one. Finally, after thirty-three minutes they declared him dead and signed a death certificate. The infant's body was then given to family members to hold, in order to facilitate their grieving. As the grandmother held the body of the lifeless newborn, all of a sudden he began to move. He recovered completely and went home with an overjoyed family. In another instance, a young woman collapsed in a snowstorm and was found completely frozen the next morning. Recovery alone would have been a miracle. The medical team expected her to lose fingers, toes, and possibly even her legs, which were severely damaged from frostbite. A prayer circle was organized by family and friends. She recovered completely, with no loss of tissue.

## On Science, Religion, and Nonlocal Reality

Accounts of mysterious healing force us to ask about the nature of the reality in which we live. Here, we may encounter one of the most majestic and awesome mysteries of all.

I argued some years ago that the power of naming is one of the crucial powers of ministry as a profession.[11] The church enacts a reality by naming the meaning of history. However, we sometimes have thought that the naming of reality provided by the church and the naming of reality provided by science are opposed. The church is therefore seen as unscientific or even opposed to science. When church leaders warn scientists against playing God, churches are perceived as being opposed to scientific advances. I want to propose a different view: that churches should welcome scientific advances, because contemporary science appears to be moving inexorably closer to a view of reality that the church has long espoused. This view is the belief that reality is nonlocal.

Belief in God and in the power of prayer suggests an understanding of reality in which there is a primary interconnectedness of life with life. In such a view, the harms that befall one person diminish others and the joys of one spill over to affect others, even at considerable distance. This implies that reality is nonlocal, not confined to time and space. Is this notion of fundamental connectedness of life with life just a nice theological vision that bears no relationship to hard scientific facts? Quite to the contrary, this view is, in fact, precisely what some recent scientific discoveries are leading us to proclaim.

Physician Larry Dossey has been studying the power of prayer in medicine for a number of years. Dossey began his medical career in a purely scientific vein, giving up his Christian faith in order to be a "good" scientist. However, when research findings suggested that love, empathy, and an attitude of prayerfulness actually have scientifically measurable results, he experienced a conversion and became convinced that to withhold prayer from his patients was to withhold a potent healing force. He returned to a faith-full way of doing medicine, incorporating prayer into his work.[12]

Dossey suggests that we have left behind the era of "physicalist" medicine, where we assumed that bodies were independent of mind and spirit. Not only have we begun to stress the interconnection between mind and body within the individual, we also have begun to understand that there are connections between and among individuals that have actual physical effects.[13] Studies of twins and of others in close relation show that when one person feels pain, the other actually feels the pain too, even when the two persons are separated by distance.[14] Other research reports that some people can make accurate medical diagnoses even though they cannot see or touch or talk to the persons they are diagnosing.[15] Still other studies show that by using mental imagery, people can change the physical reactions of others at a distance.

Most intriguing to me are some studies from the Princeton Engineering Anomalies Research lab.[16] In these studies, a machine was programmed to generate electronic pulses in a random pattern. Without touching the machine—indeed, without even being in the same room—people were able to shift the pattern from the random sequence for which the machine was originally programmed into a nonrandom pattern, simply by willing it to happen. The power of the mind extends beyond the sympathetic reactions of twins to include not only unrelated people, but also animals, plants, microorganisms, and even machines! Sometimes it does indeed seem that we have entered the twilight zone.

Such studies have led Dossey to conclude that "empathy somehow connects distant organisms."[17] There is instantaneous communication across huge gaps of space; and there is even communication across time. (Studies have shown that we can influence events before and after they have happened.)[18] I grew up in a world that was perceived as being bounded by space and time, so it is still difficult for me to comprehend what this means. But it does seem that modern physics is moving toward an understanding of the world that is nonlocal, not limited by space and time. What James Frazer once called "contagious magic" may, in fact, exist: things that have once been in contact with each other seem always to remain affected by whatever happens to the other. It appears that the world is indeed interconnected, as many religious faiths have claimed. Instead of religion needing to catch up to science, science has needed to catch up to religion![19]

Christian faith has always had a belief in a nonlocal reality—a God who transcends time and space, a Spirit who moves in mysterious ways, an Advent that not only entered history, but in whose light both past and future are radically revised. Such mysteries of faith often have been taken to be nonscientific. But as science moves toward ever more sophisticated understandings of how the universe works, the concept of nonlocal reality seems to be coming into its own scientifically. The gap between faith and science is narrowing, not because we are giving up on faith, but because both faith and science are finding new ways to describe ultimate reality.

## The Interconnections

We have, then, two types of wonder: wonder*ing* and wonder*ful*. We have scientific curiosity and the desire to know on the one hand, mystery and a sense of awe on the other. Although they are different, these two are deeply connected to each other, and the connections go in both directions.

On the one hand, the curiosity that gives rise to the desire to know—to wonder*ing*—may be an important ingredient in spiritual aliveness that allows the sense of awe and mystery—the wonder*ful*. In his reflections on mental health, M. Scott Peck suggests that curiosity is intimately linked with the ability to have a taste for mystery, and that both are an important antidote to the apathy that characterizes the mentally unhealthy.[20] Peck goes so far as to suggest that one of the forms that mental illness can take is the inability to tolerate mystery, to sustain wonder.[21] While all of us want to know, to explain, to gain some control over the fluctuations and forces in our lives, the desire to have everything neatly boxed up may be itself a form of pathology.

The convergence between science and faith holds a potential danger. We may be tempted to think that mysteries are things to be harnessed and controlled in the same way that science tries to harness and control nature. Dossey warns, however, that "so far no one has been able to demonstrate that cancer or any other disease will predictably disappear by using prayer, meditation, or any psychological or spiritual method."[22] While prayer is effective, it remains mysterious—it is not something we can use simply to change what we wish. Dossey suggests that the most powerful and effective prayer may not be focused on the particular thing that we want changed in the world, but may be instead the affirmation "thy will be done." He describes his findings about spirituality and health as "a great mystery . . . in the strongest possible sense—something unknowable, something essentially beyond human understanding."[23]

On the other hand, wonder in the sense of mystery may also be crucial for genuine scientific discovery. To be an explorer, Peck suggests, one has to have a taste for mystery.[24] Wonder in the sense of curiosity catalyzes wonder in the sense of mystery. If we never want to know how something works, if we never wonder about it in this way, will we have the capacity to see it as wonderful? Peck suggests that people who use religion to shut out mystery are in danger of closing down their spiritual maturity.[25] The more locked in to particular ways of seeing we become, the less likely we are to perceive the actual nature of reality. Sittler cautions that "the mind filled with excitements of what [we] do with the components of the world works to blunt . . . astonishment before the fact that there is a world to do something with."[26] Scientists can become so filled with the minutiae of science that they fail to perceive the mystery of the whole. For example, in our quest to map and sequence all the genes in the human body, we must not forget that the very existence of that body is wonder-full.[27]

The more we are struck by the awe, the mystery, the majesty of what we study—the more we are able to behold it rather than just to see it—the more likely we are to open ourselves up to letting it speak to us. For example, Barbara McClintock developed notions of genetics that defied all the logic of the central dogma of the genetics of her day. The central dogma was that no information from outside could ever penetrate the inheritable genetic message.[28] Based on what she called a "love" of her corn plants, or a "feeling for the organism," McClintock's attentiveness to her corn plants led her to believe that they changed their genes in response to their environment. She thus proposed a theory of transposition of genes, or "jumping genes," for which she was many years later awarded the Nobel Prize.

McClintock did not just *see* her corn plants, she *beheld* them. They became real to her. She spoke of them as her friends, utterly defying the conventions of scientific discourse of her day. In reflecting on McClintock's work, Evelyn Fox Keller proposes precisely that McClintock was led to a view of genetic reality as nonlocal: "McClintock's work on transposition required the admission of nonlocal, or global, effects."[29] Significantly, it was a form of meditation or prayer that led to some of McClintock's most important hypotheses. As Evelyn Fox Keller tells the story, McClintock was frustrated by her inability to see the transposition of genes under the microscope. She retreated to sit under a eucalyptus tree and meditate. "There she 'worked on herself.' When she felt she was ready, she returned to the microscope, and the chromosomes were now to be seen."[30] An ability to understand reality as nonlocal—the same ability that is implied in belief in God or in the healing power of prayer, the same ability implied in the forms of meditation used in many religious communities—may be a prerequisite for certain kinds of scientific insight.

Curiosity and awe are connected. It is my conviction that the church needs both, and that both will bring us closer to God. It is also my conviction that science and religion do not work against each other, but instead may be converging on an appreciation of the mysteries of nonlocal reality. Nonetheless, there is a danger that we will so stress the marvels of modern science and its wondering that we will neglect the marvels of faith and its wonder. There is a danger that we will try to control the wonders, rather than to stand before them in a state of awe and reverence. The question, then, is what sparks wonder? How do we keep ourselves wonder*ing* and wonder*ful*?

## Everyday Apathy and Holy Antidotes:
## Wrinkles in Time

Some years ago, Madeleine L'Engle wrote an award-winning children's book, *A Wrinkle in Time*.[31] The book is about time travel, an idea that has always fascinated humans in the West. To travel backward or forward in time, to reposition oneself into one's favorite era and live there instead of here—such fantasies are not merely a way of defying the historical limits into which we are born. They are also a way of stretching the spirit and imagination, and of proclaiming something both time-less and time-full about ourselves. I propose that wonder comes about from creating wrinkles in time—moments and spaces where time stands still or disappears or takes on a new, pregnant character. Time becomes *kairos* rather than *chronos*.

*Chronos* is time as measured by the watch. *Chronos* can be counted. *Kairos*, by contrast, is immeasurable. It is the fullness of time, the ripeness of time, the richness of time, in which things do not simply "happen," but "come to pass." Most of the time we live chronologically, chained to the watches worn on our wrists and the clocks ringing alarms morning, noon, and night. Yet humans do not measure or remember time only by the clock or calendar. "That was the year of the tornado." "It was just after my father died." "No, it must have been about two years before they got married." We do not measure time only by the flow of clock or calendar, but also by events that give meaning to our lives. This is *kairos*. Part of the wonder of God, part of the wonder of church, is that time has different meaning in this context.

It is these wrinkles in time, these moments when time stands still or takes on new meaning, that allow wonder in our lives. In the time-fullness of *kairos*, time stands still and we slow down or speed up enough to wonder *about* things and to wonder *at* them. Achieving *kairos* instead of *chronos* is partly a matter of perspective. It has to do with learning to behold rather than merely to see the world. What works for one will not necessarily work for another here. Many have spoken of how disaster or impending death gives new perspective. But is it necessary to wait for disaster to strike in order to experience wrinkles in time? What might the church do to enable these moments of *kairos* for us?

In a paradox that Reinhold Niebuhr would have loved, I propose that we can create kairos in two ways that move in seemingly opposite directions: (1) by slowing down and attending to the still, small voice of God, and (2) by making a joyful noise unto the Lord.

## *The Still, Small Voice of God (1 Kings 19:11-12)*

In *Three Mile an Hour God*, Kosuke Koyama similarly proposes that in order to find *kairos*, we may have to slow down. We are always in a hurry, rushing to beat the clock, trying to increase efficiency. A country-western song put it this way: "I'm in a hurry to get things done; I rush and rush until life's no fun." God does not always hurry. Koyama suggests that God spent forty years in the wilderness teaching the Israelites one lesson.[32] When I joined a church twenty years ago, the scriptural passage that was chosen for me was from Psalm 27: "Wait upon the Lord." For me, that is probably one of the hardest messages. But I do know that in my rushing, I tend to shut out God.

My students know that I am a great lover of Winnie the Pooh. Pooh sits and waits until a "hum" comes to him. Hums are not, he suggests, things that you can go and get, but things that get you. There are insights to be had, but they cannot always be had by trying to go and get them; sometimes, they come from quiet waiting. When Barbara McClintock wanted to understand her corn plants and why they did not appear to follow the laws of genetic mutation, she sat down under a tree and meditated.[33] It was through meditation that the insight came to her that perhaps the genes actually jumped from one location to another. Her discovery took six years of patient observation of the same corn plants. It could not be hurried. She was in the process of letting reality speak to her, instead of imposing her own views on reality. If we are to create wrinkles in time, to incarnate moments of *kairos* in the midst of *chronos*, we probably need to slow down, to wait upon God.

Part of waiting is silence. Protestant churches tend to be full of words. But as Catherine de Hueck Doherty (founder of Friendship House in Harlem) puts it, "Love often expresses itself best in an infinite and tender silence, especially when dealing with those deeply wounded by life or by the indifference of their brethren in Christ."[34] The great mystic Meister Eckhart is said to have observed that "nothing in all creation is so like God as stillness." Silence is respectful—it is respectful toward others and toward God. The Quakers have long known the great gift of silence, making room for the Spirit to move. I remember hearing Howard Thurman speak once. He stood silently before the room and gathered the Spirit in before he spoke. It was palpable. The audience could feel it. When Thurman spoke, his words were filled with the power of the Spirit. They inspired wonder. The silence became a part of the power of the word.

Koyama speaks of the time when he stood on Wilmot Pass in the fjord lands of New Zealand. There, he says, "I found myself in the silence of a primeval world."[35] The silence, Koyama suggests, "purified my soul." And he notes that simultaneously with the sense of purification came the sense of being connected to everything and responsible for others.

Another part of waiting is ruminating. We tend to live on fast food: quickly made, quickly bought, quickly eaten, and quickly forgotten. Perhaps we need to take time to chew. Cows ruminate.[36] They chew things over and over. We tend to want to chew things up and spit them out as fast as we can. Yet I know that when I reread a book, I always get something new out of it. Mulling the same thing over and over can be quite enlightening. A sermon series on the same biblical text that allows it to be redigested each week until it is thoroughly chewed might provide sweet cream.

The excitement generated by wonder is not to be confused with giddily rushing from one new thing to another, ever seeking new experiences in a manner that can become addictive. Couples who have been together for a long time and remain in love experience wonder in the midst of familiarity. Thus, wonder can be the deepening of something old and familiar, holding and turning it until the light strikes it differently and it shines in unfamiliar ways. Like a kaleidoscope, the old and familiar may have the same ingredients but look different each time it is viewed.

The first avenue to *kairos*, then, is stillness, waiting, anticipating, ruminating, cogitating. It involves letting the universe speak to us rather than imposing our understanding on the universe. It involves a stance of reverence before that which is deep and mysterious and wonder*ful*, and it also involves active wonder*ing* that pushes us to look again, to want to know, to want to experience.

## *Making a Joyful Noise*

Slowing down does not mean lacking energy. I've been in churches where the pastor or lay leader welcomed the congregation in such lackluster style that my energy level fell through the floor. Do we really believe that God will sustain us? Do we really enjoy church? Do we really wonder at the mystery of God's love and grace? If so, it should show in the lilt of our voices, the lift of our bodies, the spring in our step. "Wow" makes us reverent and hushed, but it also fills us with excitement, with eagerness. We are awed and humbled by what we see ahead, but we are also eager to rush in and experience it. Silence is not apathy but respectful walking, watching, and waiting. Wonder does not preclude making a joyful noise unto God.

Indeed, the second avenue to *kairos* may lie precisely in an abundance of spirit that comes from expanding the senses, being fully alive, and stretching ourselves. I grew up partly in the Lutheran tradition, and the richness of the music and liturgical form in that tradition still draws me in a way that the dry silence and unregulated liturgy of many Protestant churches does not. Anyone who has attended an Easter candlelight mass in a Roman Catholic church knows that the power of words to reach the human spirit can pale beside ritual and nonverbal forms of worship.

The power of words lies in their ability to evoke images which in turn evoke whole worlds of meaning. The cross is not just two sticks, one slightly longer than the other, set at right angles. The cross is a powerful symbol of suffering and joy, death and resurrection, judgment and hope. It is a nonverbal word. In Calvinist traditions, we are sometimes so word-oriented that we forget the power of images, of silence, of symbols, of scent, of sound, of taste, of touch. Yet the senses have immense power to lift our spirits into wonder. Let us take a brief excursus into the senses.

## Sight

Western cultures have become visually oriented cultures. We use visual imagery to indicate knowledge: "I see" means "I comprehend." Of all the senses, then, we are most likely to stress the visual. We put flowers on the altar. We change the colors of our altar cloths. We make sure the cross is visible, front and center. Our pulpits are elevated, so that we can see as well as hear the preacher. Our choirs sit in the front of the church, dressed in bright robes. We process. We recess. In an old church, we may have beautiful stained-glass windows. In newer churches, careful use of modern stained glass might throw patches of colored light across the pews or onto the altar. In a bold church, we hang bright banners on the walls. Some churches are now experimenting with dance and movement. All these things we do to enhance our experience of worship, our encounter with mystery, our sense of wonder.

## "Seeing Voices"

Once in a Boston subway station, I watched two people having an animated conversation. Their gestures were so lively and they seemed to be enjoying each other so much that I slipped closer to listen in, hoping to catch a snatch of what enlivened them so. Only when I was within a few feet did I realize, to my chagrin, that they were not speaking with their voices. They were signing. Hands were flying, bodies were being positioned in an intricate and beautiful dance that mesmerized me. I was, as Oliver Sacks puts it in his study of the deaf community and the neuropsychology of sign language, seeing voices.[37]

Sign language is a spatial and architectural language. Studies show that children—whether hearing or deaf—who learn and practice sign language do better on spatial skills than do children raised with only spoken languages.[38] Signers live in four-dimensional reality, using three-dimensional space as well as time to communicate. Spoken language is one-dimensional, having only time and linear relationship of words to indicate meaning. The use of space as well as time opens up vast possibilities for communicating the Word. Anyone who has ever witnessed the grace of sign language can readily appreciate what Sacks calls its "singular appropriateness for religious worship."[39]

Of particular interest to me was Sacks' finding that, while there is no universal sign language, signers coming from different languages soon learned easily to communicate with each other. In 1989, an international conference of some five thousand deaf people from eighty different countries began with dozens of sign languages. Yet within a week, communication among different nationalities was relatively easy.[40] I lived in Montreal for almost two years, yet I never developed any real facility at speaking French to my neighbors. I envy the ease with which those using sign languages are able to transcend their linguistic differences. If we believe that Babel is a curse, we may have something to learn from the visual experience of seeing voices.

I am not suggesting that all churches learn sign language. I confess to being skeptical sometimes when I am asked to learn a few simple hand movements to accompany songs in church. I have been known positively to resist being asked to stand in a "wave" or dance in church aisles. Yet I also know that there is a power in nonverbal words that lends wonder to our worship.

## Sound

Ever since Norman Cousins wrote about healing himself through laughter,[41] we have become increasingly aware of the powerful link between laughter and health. Somewhere I read that singing is like laughing multiplied ten times. Certainly, in some forms of Eastern medicine, sounds are used to heal both body and mind.[42] Music reaches the soul on levels where almost nothing else can. Thus, it can be an important generator of wonder.

Some years ago, I had the privilege of going to China with a delegation of church leaders. Although our delegation spoke no Chinese, we often communicated with people there by singing hymns. We would sing a stanza of an old favorite; they might respond with the second stanza or with another old favorite. In this way, we came to understand how much we shared even though there were language and cultural differences. Moreover, we were told that the music is one of the major reasons the churches in China are overflowing.[43] Successful churches—such as Glide Memorial in

San Francisco—are often churches where the rafters ring with music. Music is a particularly powerful expression of faith.[44]

This music is not always traditional. At Glide, the music may be gospel, blues, rock, jazz, or modern, as well as traditional hymns. Feet are tapping, hands are clapping, and there is joy in the church. I find it sometimes overwhelming, but always wonderful.

Yet precisely here we come to a problem. The importance of music means that if the church wants to reach new communities, it must use new music.[45] New music doesn't always speak to old-timers, however. In an effort to develop adequate theology, some denominations have retired old favorites such as "Onward Christian Soldiers." For some people, this means that their favorite hymns are disappearing. They miss those hymns, and something feels as though it is missing in church.[46] The Montreal *Gazette* of 13 April 1995 printed a letter telling of a recent experience in which the minister at an ecumenical service allowed the congregation to choose the final hymn. The author reported that "a little old lady with a twinkle in her eye" quickly proposed "Onward Christian Soldiers," and "we sang with enough fervor to tumble the walls of Jericho."[47]

On the other hand, many young people today were not raised in churches. "Onward Christian Soldiers," "The Old Rugged Cross," "I Would Be True," "Love Divine, All Loves Excelling," "Joyful, Joyful We Adore Thee"—all these and almost all traditional hymns carry little or no meaning to today's fifteen-to thirty-year-olds. Like old-timers in the church, they find that the soul is expressed through music.[48] However, the music of young people is a different music. It is a music almost never heard in church. No wonder the young people are not there, if the music that expresses their soul is not there.

What should churches do in face of this generation gap? I propose that we follow the advice of Paul, who said, "I became as a Jew . . . I became as one under the law" (1 Cor. 9:20). If it is the reign of God that matters, then the form of the church that matters is the form that will facilitate the emergence of that reign. It may be crucial that we not throw the baby out with the bath water, but it is just as crucial that we not cling to the bath water simply because the baby has been soaked in it! If Paul could become as a Jew in order to reach the Jews, then why should the church not become a riot of music in order to reach different groups? Drums, bamboo, bagpipe, organ, guitar, flute, trombone—let the rafters ring! The task of the church is not to resist the new, but to come to understand the historical limits of the old and to search diligently for all modes of communication with God.

## Smell

Who doesn't love the smell of a live Christmas tree? Whether pine or spruce, a living tree in our living space creates a feast for the olfactory glands. More than many of us realize, scent has the ability to evoke memories, to recreate space, to embody joy and wonder in our midst.

My mother baked bread only rarely. But who could forget the smell of fresh baked bread filling a house, inviting, soothing, calming, centering, and energizing all at once? In Montreal, I lived near an Italian bakery. The smell was so tantalizing that I could scarcely walk by without wanting to go in and beg for a morsel. Alas, this bakery supplied restaurants and did not sell directly to the public! But just walking on the street outside was a treat.

Protestant churches historically have made little of the sense of smell, unlike Catholic and Orthodox churches, where incense may be routinely used to enhance worship. Incense makes me sneeze, and I am not advocating the use of it in all churches. But when was the last time you stopped to ask how your church smells? What feelings and memories were evoked the last time the church was decorated with pine boughs or Easter lilies? Did you feel a bit more joyful walking into that space? Scent can do much to enhance our sense of wonder and our encounter with the divine.

## Taste

Like smell, taste has a powerful ability to evoke memories. Let me tell you a story.

Shortly after I moved to Berkeley, California, many years ago, I discovered the local Egg Shop and Apple Press, a restaurant chain that made fabulous omelettes and fresh apple cider. One day I tried a dish of something they called Swiss ice cream. Instantly, I was flooded with memories of being a little girl. I could not place the flavor, and it haunted me. I consumed dish after dish of ice cream, trying to figure out the flavor that was evoking the edge of a memory from deep in my childhood. Finally, I got it: Ovaltine! The flavor was of malted chocolate milk, and it reminded me of those wonderful Sunday evenings when we would have waffles and Ovaltine for supper.

Anyone who has ever tasted a tomato picked fresh from the vine knows that it bears no relationship to the taste of hothouse or store-bought tomatoes. Corn picked from the stalk and thrown into boiling water within thirty seconds tastes completely different from corn that has sat for three days on a grocer's shelf. Taste matters!

When Jesus broke bread and gave it to his disciples, it was undoubt-edly a different bread than the bread that my mother baked on those rare and wonderful occasions. No doubt Jesus' bread was unleavened, heavy, made of coarse grains rather than refined flour, and very likely chewy rather than melt-in-your-mouth. One church I attended used tortillas one Sunday. Pita bread, pumpernickel, sourdough (a San Francisco favorite!), Wheat Thins, cheese sticks—does it really matter what we use, so long as there is enough taste to tantalize our senses, to shock our sensibilities into recognition that it is both a very routine and a very special thing that we are doing when we break bread together?

I once heard someone say with scorn that he had witnessed a Communion service in which potato chips and Coca-Cola were used. He was disgusted. Would Jesus have been disgusted? I think not. Jesus used bread and wine because it was what was available in his culture, but there is nothing sacred about bread and wine per se.[49] When young people sit down to pizza and Coke, are they not, in fact, sharing in a kind of communion meal? If the sharing of food makes them more thoughtful toward one another, more ready to serve one another, more wonder-full, then it is not contrary to the will of God. All of the common things of this world have the capacity to commu-nicate God to us; whether they do so depends on how we use them.[50]

## Touch

Just as Protestant churches have lost their focus on smell and taste, so they tend to lose their focus on touch. We have no statues for the faithful to caress on their way into church. We have few traditions of kneeling before God.[51] We have lost both the joy and the pain of physical exertion as a means of communicating with God.

Outside the magnificent Oratoire St. Joseph in Montreal is a pil-grim's path of more than a hundred steps. One side is reserved for those approaching on their knees—a long, slow, painful climb. Only a few make that climb on hard concrete, bending and bruising their knees but possibly straightening their spirits on the way.[52] Kosuke Koyama writes powerfully about the importance of such a slow, preeminently physical approach to God.[53] Pilgrims, he says, used to be required to take their shoes off before walking the long steps to the Shwe Dagon Pagoda in Burma; for the benefit of tourists, an elevator was later installed. Shoes off, Koyama stood in the elevator, neither pilgrim nor tourist, wondering if God could be approached in this manner.

If the physically arduous can be a means of wonder—a way to open up the wonderful in our lives—so can the physically comforting. Touch can heal. Just as the healing power of prayer remains a mystery, so does the healing power of touch. While not all churches will embrace practices such as the kiss of peace, it is important to consider the power of touch and what might be appropriate ways to include it in worship and in the life of the church.

So we have sight, sound, smell, taste, and touch—five senses to enliven our worship, five ways of making a joyful noise unto God. The senses are what we use when we are wonder*ing* and they are also avenues to the wonder*ful*. They can fill us with delight and joy, make us see things differently, open our hearts and minds to God. They are, therefore, a very important part of being the Body of Christ that tries to live the gospel. We also have stillness and silence, the gathering in of what is beyond us and beyond our comprehension. Both are modes of wonder*ing* and of being reverent before the wonder*ful*. But alone, they are not enough. In the next chapter, we turn to the Word which anchors our worship.

# WORD

---
✿
---

A dear friend moved recently after more than twenty-five years of living in one area. The move was necessitated by her husband's work, but it felt to her like going into exile. It cut her off from her community of friends and colleagues, it placed her in a location where finding work in her specialty would be nearly impossible, and it came just at a time when she was dealing with a life-threatening illness that limited her mobility and made it difficult for her to go out into the community and find new friends and colleagues. It was, in short, a devastating experience.

It was with great joy, then, that she reported that she had found a new church home. When I asked her why this church felt right to her, she replied, "I felt at home in this congregation because the word was well articulated and the worship was inclusive and creative." In the next chapter, I will look at the question of inclusive worship; here, I will focus on the articulation of the word. As it was for my friend, it is often the articulation of the word that brings people to church.

Ever since Luther proclaimed *sola scriptura* and chastised the Roman Catholic church for the ways in which he believed its rituals and practices had kept people from the Word of God, Protestants have seen themselves as people of the Word. In Reformation tradition,[1] preaching is central to worship. While denominations differ in their stress on liturgy, ritual, and ceremony, all Protestant traditions tend to emphasize the sermon and proclamation of the Word. As it

---

would be true of many other Protestants, so it is true of me: I go to church to hear the Word of God.[2] But what is this word?

"In the beginning was the Word, and the Word was with God, and the Word was God" (John 1:1). In Christian community and worship, the words that we speak are intended to convey the Word that is beyond speech. Already, then, we have a dilemma, for our words are never adequate, nor could they ever be! Moreover, words can be both spoken and unspoken. Words come to us in church in sermons, prayers, hymns, litanies, responsive readings, church announcements, bulletins, and in the welcome or greeting of fellow worshipers. They also come in altar cloths, body postures, handshakes. All these words are important for conveying the Word. Moreover, nonverbal words are often as important as the verbal ones. Does a newcomer sit alone in church? Words of welcome can pale beside the act of ignoring someone's presence. In the next chapter, I will look at some of the nonverbal ways in which we communicate. So while I focus here on the preaching of the Word that is often central to Protestant worship, it is important to remember that the articulation of the Word takes many forms in the church. If the church is to be renewed, many words must be renewed.[3]

Speech is a twofold act: of speaking and of listening. Each of us brings something different to our hearing of the word that is spoken. As a teacher, I know how often I think I have said one thing and my students have heard something else. I therefore do not envy preachers the task of trying to speak a word that will resonate with so many different listeners. Yet there are words that I long to hear in church. Some pastors long to speak them, and they need to know that the words will not fall on deaf ears. They are words of *conviction, passion,* and *remembrance.*

## *Conviction*

### *Being Convicted*

In *Vanishing Boundaries,* Dean Hoge and his colleagues tackle the question of "the religion of mainline Protestant baby boomers."[4] They propose that there are four main "commodities" that boomers want from the church: (1) religious education for children and support for family life, (2) personal support and reassurance, (3) social contacts and a sense of community, and (4) inspiration and spiritual guidance around questions of ultimate meaning.[5] If this is true, then I am hardly a typical boomer! I have no children and, therefore, do not seek from the church support for family life and religious education for children. For more than five years I was one of the few straight members of a mostly gay and lesbian church; I understood that church to be my worshiping community, but I did not use it as my primary social community. While I developed friends in the church, I never used it as a primary place for personal support and reassurance, since I have a rather wide circle of friends and acquaintances to whom I turn for personal support. Three of the four categories that Hoge lists do not appear to fit me well.

The fourth does, with some nuancing. I seek from church inspiration and guidance on questions of ultimate meaning. I seek a holy antidote for the apathy of everyday life.[6] Like the baby boomers whom Hoge described, I want worship to be uplifting and empowering, drawing me away from petty concerns so I can remember the larger picture.

Indeed, it is precisely this larger picture that I really want from church. I do not need church to be a community where I find all my friends, or where I am universally liked. I do need it to be a place where I am challenged to remember that which is of ultimate importance in human life. The type of community that forms a church and that is formed by the biblical story is important not only because it is a *privilege*, as Bonhoeffer claims, but also because that community provides an *accountability structure*. The church is not there simply to meet my needs or offer me support, but to hold me accountable precisely for those things that are difficult for me to do but which have ultimate meaning.

Because accountability and the "big picture" are central, the term that I associate with hearing the word of God is the term *convicted*. For me, no matter how well articulated the word is in terms of the beauty of the phrasing, the word is not sufficiently well articulated if it is not a convicting word. Henry Sloane Coffin once said that the word of God "comforts the afflicted and afflicts the comfortable." Because I am one of the comfortable, I do not go to church so much for comfort as to be discomforted—reminded of that which I ought to be living and most likely am not. I go to church to be convicted by the Word.

Because we often think of convicted only in connection with the guilt and innocence of those tried by the legal system, it is important to clarify what I mean. The dictionary offers as definitions: (1) to be "convinced of error or sinfulness" and (2) to be "compelled to admit the truth."[7] To these I would add: (3) to be reminded of my roots, of God's ways, of what it is that I should be doing with my life, of *who* I am and of *whose* I am, of how I fall short of the vision and call of God, of how I am nonetheless forgiven, of how I might get back on the track to which I am called.

This composite definition is what it means to me to be convicted. This is what hearing the Word of God entails. Going to church to hear the word is a reminder to me of God's reign and an encouragement that it does matter whether I walk in God's reign or not, whether I do justice, love mercy, and walk humbly with God. When I hear the Word of God, that word is a reminder of my failings, of my falling short of truth, of my idolatry and sinfulness, but it is also a reminder of my yearnings for truth and justice and of the power and majesty of God, who intervenes in the midst of my failings to offer rescue and to justify.

To me the most convicting passage from the New Testament is Matthew 5:23-24: "When you are offering your gift at the altar, if you remember that your brother or sister has something against you, leave your gift there before the altar and go; first be reconciled to your brother or sister, and then come and offer your gift." This is a very discomforting (and much neglected!) word for those of us who are relatively well off. But it is a word with power. This passage tells me that worship depends on right relationship. In a world in which there is injustice, in a world in which others have something "against" me, in a world in which people are alienated from each other, there are impediments to approaching the altar. It tells me that something is missing from my worship unless I have tried to set things right with my neighbor. Only then can praise of God begin.

For example, the witness of the Bible on matters of economic justice seems absolutely clear: the consistent prophetic message is the denunciation of people who feed off the lives of the poor and trample them into the dust. Yet I resist giving a few pennies to the homeless people I see on the streets. In spite of my comfort, in spite of my intellectual belief that my comfort comes at the price of others' discomfort, I often grumble or, if I give, I give grudgingly. Hearing the word—hearing Matthew 5:23-24—brings me back to reality. It convicts me.

I was on my way to church one night when I realized that I was out of money. I decided to stop quickly at the automatic teller machine on my way to church. It was early December, the beginning of Advent, my favorite season of the church year. Standing outside the bank was a person bundled so heavily against the cold that I could not tell whether it was a man or woman. This person was holding a sign that read, "Homeless. Will work for food." Matthew 5:23-24 leaped into my mind, and I could not continue on to church when my neighbor was standing there cold, shivering, hungry, and homeless.

Thus began a three-year relationship with Mary and Tom.[8] Mary and Tom were on the street for most of the first year that I knew them. They were on drugs, as are many street people. Their children had been taken away and put in foster homes. They had little hope and even fewer possessions. Mary and Tom are the poor, the outcast, the marginalized. People like them can be found in every city in every country of the world.

I hired Mary and Tom to do whatever jobs I could find, mostly menial tasks such as cleaning and weeding. It was not always a smooth relationship: my backyard was destroyed because Tom could not distinguish weeds from plants, my vacuum cleaner was inadvertently demolished, most of my garden tools disappeared, and some of my jewelry was stolen. At times I wondered if it wouldn't have been easier to give Mary and Tom money every time I saw them on the corner rather than try to offer them a genuine "new beginning." But justice requires that people be offered respect and an opportunity to improve their lot, and respect does not come through handouts alone.[9]

Although my losses were many during this three-year period, there were compensations. There was the time Mary and Tom proudly told me that they had saved their money for three months in order to make a security deposit on an apartment so they could finally get off the streets. There was the time they took their precious pennies and bought me a single red rose—a gift more beautiful than any large bouquet I have ever received, and reminiscent of the widow giving two coins in contrast to the larger offerings of the wealthy. There were many times that Mary and Tom prayed for my mother when she was very ill and nearly died. Although it was a rocky relationship, it had its elements of mutuality and friendship.

Mary and Tom were a risk. But without taking that risk, I could not come to the altar of God. The Word of God is there to remind me of how it is that I am meant to live and what the human community as a whole is meant to be. Unless I turn a deaf ear to the prophets, unless I close my heart to the message of Matthew, I cannot bring gifts to the altar while ignoring my neighbor's needs and the historical injustices on which those needs are so often based. This is the discomfort that the Word brings. The renewal of the church depends on a willingness to preach and to hear this discomforting word, the word of conviction that brings the God of justice into our midst.

## Connection

However, my feeble efforts to help Tom and Mary were just that—feeble efforts. I never took Mary and Tom into my own home, even when they were homeless. I never committed myself to care for them forever, in covenant fashion. I never found a way to get them off drugs and into the kinds of rehabilitation programs that I know they need. (I tried, but did not succeed.)

Precisely here is where I need the church. Our streets are groaning with homeless people. Hands reach out to us whenever we enter a major city. So many people are in need that my little efforts are like drops of water falling on a rock. Yet the more drops of water that are joined together, the faster the rock will be worn away. I need the community of church not simply to provide the context in which I might be personally convicted, but to provide the context in which those convictions can be joined to the convictions of others and social change can be effected. As a worldwide institution, the church is powerful indeed. It represents the possibility of putting many little streams together into a raging river of justice. This vision is what keeps me connected to the church.

The church and the words I hear there are important not only for convicting me, but also for connecting me—to others who also do their feeble bit for justice, to ways of thinking that will help to transform the unjust structures in which we live, and to the multiple links between the privileges of my life and the pains of others' lives.

We live in a world full of injustice and oppression.[10] We inherit a system that we would like to think is fair—full of equal opportunity and equal treatment. But the data overwhelm us: if things are fair, if opportunities are equal, then why are our cities filling with rage, why are handguns proliferating, and why are ordinary citizens scared to go out of their houses at night? If things are fair, why does a recent study of 80,000 federal court convictions reveal a disturbing pattern of blacks routinely being given longer sentences than whites convicted of similar crimes?[11] No, our world is not fair. It is full of injustice, exploitation, and oppression.

Most of the time, we are not directly the cause of those injustices. I had never seen Mary and Tom until the night I found Mary shivering in the cold holding her sign. It might seem, then, that their plight is beyond my responsibility. Of course, the early church fathers would have been absolutely clear that their plight was not beyond my responsibility: consistently, the church fathers saw giving alms not as a matter of charity but as a matter of justice—of returning to the poor what is rightfully theirs. "Are you not a robber?" asks Basil the Great. "That bread which you keep belongs to the hungry."[12] Ambrose concurs: "This is justice: that one restore to the needy."[13] For the early church fathers, giving to the poor was restoring what was already rightfully theirs; failing to give it was robbery.

The early church fathers did what contemporary feminists call "making the connections."[14] To make the connections is to see how entire systems work together to create and sustain justice or injustice. A startling example of making connections comes from Richard Preston's riveting book, *The Hot Zone*. Preston points out that the HIV virus was carried down the Kinshasa highway from the African rain forest, and he suggests that "the paving of the Kinshasa highway affected almost every person on earth, and turned out to be one of the most important events of the twentieth century. It has already cost at least ten million lives."[15] The famous slogan from the rise of feminism in this century is "the personal is political." To assert that the personal is political is to claim that what happens to us on a presumably personal and private level can never be disconnected from what happens in structures and systems. Just so is the death of my dear friend Jim directly connected to the paving of a highway in Africa.

Another example is the distressing impoverishment of elderly women in our society. A number of factors contribute to that poverty. Having stayed home to raise their children, women often entered the job market late. They therefore accumulated less pension during their working years, and this affects their retirement income. They may have dropped out of school to support their families or their husbands' education and, hence, entered the job market with fewer skills, having to take lower paying work; this, too, affects their salary, retirement, and pension benefits. In other words, women's personal plight of poverty is not unrelated to social expectations and policies—to the expectations that women should stay home to raise children, that women don't really "need" to work and can be paid less than men for equivalent work, that it is fair to correlate pensions with length of employment, and so on.[16] Just so will Mary's and Tom's plight be connected—albeit perhaps indirectly—to my fortune.

Embedded in the biblical word is this wisdom of connections that we need today. Biblical thought is organic thought. The Bible sees everything in relation to everything else. Biblical authors knew well that the wealth of some is bought at the price of the poverty of others. Their stories are replete with corrections for these gaps and injustices: with a Sabbath year in which slaves are freed, a jubilee year in which debts are remitted so that the stranglehold of cycles of poverty is broken, with calls to restore fourfold what has been unjustly taken from the poor, with the forgiveness of the sins of the past so that new beginnings can abound. The good news is a turning upside down of expectations: the slaves will be freed, the mighty will be brought down and the lowly lifted up, the valleys will be exalted and the mountains laid low. In God's reign, the poor are blessed because they are not locked into the cycle of despair that poverty brings. The connections are understood, and they are dismantled so that new life can begin.

It is this to which the church is called in order to find life-producing tension in the in-between times. Part of the task of articulating the Word, part of what it means to articulate the Word well, is to make these connections, to help us see how pieces of the puzzle fit together. To make the connections will sometimes produce *metanoia,* or radical change.

When I was a graduate student, I worked one summer for the Center for Law and Medicine at Boston University. My team of five students included a law student, a pre-med student, an economist, a metallurgist, and me. We were given ten weeks in which to choose a topic in medical ethics and write a report on it. After eight weeks of haggling, we finally chose our topic: prenatal diagnosis of Down syndrome. In a frantic effort to meet our ten-week deadline for the final report, I spent most of the next two weeks in the medical library reading everything I could find on Down syndrome. What I found turned my life around.

Prior to that study, I had shared a view unfortunately all too common in the 1960s—the view that children with Down syndrome were hopelessly retarded, would never reach a mental age greater than two, and were a tragedy and a burden to their families. Once I began my research, however, I discovered that almost all the studies of children with Down syndrome had been done in institutions for the retarded. It doesn't take a genius to conjecture that their low levels of mental achievement might reflect their setting rather than the innate limitations of the children! The conclusion that children with Down syndrome are inevitably severely retarded could not be drawn from the evidence without further investigation as to possible causes.

This is left-brain, logical study of the sort that is prevalent in science and in the field of ethics. It led me to question the view of Down syndrome that was dominant at that time. It led me to being an advocate for children with Down syndrome. It changed completely the way I approached the question of prenatal diagnosis of this medical condition. It was a *metanoia.* That *metanoia* was brought about by applying the best of logical reasoning to the evidence with which I was confronted. Since that experience, I do not underestimate the power and importance of such left-brain activities. The power of making the connections for people is that conversion can happen. Even through the use of logic, deduction, inference, and other common practices of dry, dull, prose language and scientific investigation, *metanoia* is possible.[17] Making the connections, showing the logical links, and showing the lack of logical links, can be a world-transforming event.

To be a biblical word, the word spoken in church must acknowledge these connections and help us to see the ways in which the personal is political. It must connect individual struggle to corporate responsibility. This is part of what it means to speak a word of conviction.

## Conviction, Not Blame

But now readers may be nervous. "Am I responsible for everything? Am I to blame?" Yes, and no: the word of conviction deals with responsibility, but not with blame. Because the personal is political—because our neighbor's need is so often the result not simply of misfortune, but of injustice and the interlocking of systems—we have responsibility for correcting that injustice and addressing the need. Wherever there is injustice, we are called to do justice and to correct the injustice.

Still, we often associate responsibility with guilt or blame. But responsibility is not the same thing as blame. Blame implies attribution of cause. Sometimes I have caused ills in the world, and I am to blame for them. If I lie or cheat or knowingly do something to harm someone else, then I am blameworthy, and it may be appropriate for me not merely to take responsibility, but to feel guilt over my actions. But often I am not the cause and not directly to blame for the ills of the world. I did not establish slavery in the United States, I have never owned a slave, and I am not personally to blame for the many horrors of that practice. Nonetheless, I inherit a society in which slavery left its legacy and in which current problems have antecedents in historical injustices. There are connections between my well-being as a white person and the history of slavery in the United States. I am, therefore, responsible to correct, to the extent possible, the legacy of injustices that slavery left behind. I am not guilty, and I am not to blame, but I nonetheless have responsibility.[18]

The word of conviction helps us take responsibility where we should, but without making us feel guilty for those things that are beyond our personal control. It is an ethical word, not a moralizing word. The moralizing word makes us feel guilty even when we are not. Making me feel guilty will only make me resentful and resistant to the very justice that I need to do. The word of conviction, however, helps me to see the connections so I can take responsibility, but it does not weigh me down in the mire of guilt and blame.

Like a jubilee year, justice requires new beginnings. The jubilee was not popular in its day,[19] and will not be popular now, because it requires that we give up some of our securities and wealth in the interests of God's righteousness. To be convicted is to be convinced of the truth of the connections that place obligations on us. There is no need for guilt, but there is need for action to do justice.[20] The moralizing word aims at blame; the word of conviction aims at responsibility so that justice can be done. This is the word that will renew the church, speaking truth that convicts and connects us. This is the word that I want to hear.

## Language

Words themselves are problematic. Language is not only a vehicle through which we convey words of conviction and connection. It is itself a powerful carrier of justice or injustice. Language creates and frames the reality in which we live.[21] One of the legacies with which we live, unfortunately, is the legacy of injustices created by our patterns of language usage. For example, the persistent use of "black" or "dark" to mean "evil" or "bad" is an unjust language pattern. This is a place where the hearing of the word becomes crucial.

In her poignant autobiographical reflections, *Memories of God,* Roberta Bondi speaks of the "nightmares" she used to experience because she had been told that God was a heavenly Father, and she assumed that this meant God was like her earthly father. "In public prayer," she writes, "the use of the name Father would regularly fill me with a sense of inadequacy, helplessness, and depression."[22] Bondi is not alone. For many women, and for some men as well, the use of Father language for God is problematic. Through a deliberate regimen of prayer, Bondi herself was able to recapture the term *father* as a positive way of speaking about God, but she nonetheless urges that pastors be cautious in their use of this imagery and that they actively seek other names and images for God.[23]

I would go further. We live in a society in which young people increasingly come from abusive homes. Statistics on child abuse are notoriously unreliable, but there is good evidence that at least one out of every three women and one out of seven men has been sexually abused at some time early in life.[24] Some of this abuse takes place at the hands of fathers. Children who have never known a loving and trustworthy father early in life may find in the image of God as Father the loving father they never knew and always needed. Some may find this image very comforting and very welcome. But others will not. When young children have been physically, mentally, or sexually abused by their fathers, to call God "Father" can evoke very painful memories, as Bondi attests. We must be careful about our use of this term in the church. Many children will know a loving mother instead of a loving father, and may find it easier to think of God as a great Mother whose love is steadfast and endures forever.

Even for those of us who had loving earthly fathers, the constant imaging of God as Father can be limiting and problematic. If God is imaged exclusively as male, then women are excluded from the divine. As one woman put it, "To believe that God is only Father is to become aware of myself as stranger, as outsider, as alienated person, as a daughter who does not belong, who is not appointed to the marvelous destiny offered to the sons."[25] Moreover, women are excluded from leadership or full participation in the church. Little boys can play God in the church pageant, but not little girls. So begins a process of excluding and limiting what females can do and who they can be. Because God is imaged as male, those qualities associated with maleness become "divine" or more valuable than those associated with femaleness. This is particularly ironic in the Christian church, where we worship a God who comes to us as a helpless infant and of whom we presumably exalt precisely the weakness associated with the newborn infant. Yet, in the real world, we do not organize ourselves as though we value weakness, but rather as though we value stereotypical qualities of masculine control, strength, and domination. Women's works, words, and ways of being become devalued.

The imaging of God in consistently masculine terms is ethically problematic, then, because it contributes to the exclusion of women from status and full being. It has had serious detrimental consequences for women and for the church.[26] Our language for God must not only be true to God (more on this below), but must also allow people to approach God. Any language that takes away that possibility of approach is suspect at best, demonic at worst. It is for this reason that I would join most feminists in urging that we minimize the language of "Father" in the church and always ensure that such imagery is coupled with images of God as loving mother, friend, creator, sustainer, and redeemer. Since "Father" God is often "the holy presence that has nurtured the people of this church," as one pastor put it,[27] new names and faces for God may be hard for some church members to accept. The transition will take time and patience. But for those who are concerned about why some of us have left or nearly left the church, the language that we use to speak of God may be central to the answer. It is for me. I find it impossible to worship in a church where God is consistently imaged in exclusively masculine language.

## *Passion*

### *Prose and Poetry*

Some readers now are wondering what has happened to the redeemer, to the "good news." Does the language of conviction leave us stuck in legalistic imagery that implies judgment and negation? Where is the gospel message? Where is the word of forgiveness, atonement, and grace? When I suggest that the church is there to convict us, that it will discomfort those of us who are relatively well off, I do not mean to ignore the important role of comfort. Even middle-class people experience pain and need comfort. Both discomfort and comfort are, I believe, the result of hearing truth spoken. Truth has healing power, and it will often bring comfort and healing to the broken and hurting. Truth also has convicting power, and it will bring hurting and brokenness to the settled and secure. But through that hurting, healing will happen.

This is another way of saying that the word of God is a word of judgment and grace. It is a word that calls us into account, but it is also a word that lifts us out of despair. The good news is that life is stronger than death, love is stronger than hate, resurrection conquers evil. The good news is that God loves us. The good news is that God has the capacity to take all of our stumbling, our mistakes, our pettiness, our alienation, our sin and set it right. The good news is that even when the whole world reviles us, God is suffering alongside us.

To hear this word of grace, we need a language that surpasses understanding. We also need a place where the good news is lived out, a community in which the message is visible, tangible, believable. I address the issue of community in the next chapter. Here, I focus still on words. What are the words that can convey the gospel message?

They are words of poetry and passion. In *Fear and Trembling*, Søren Kierkegaard speaks of the "knight of faith" as one who learns to "express the sublime in the pedestrian absolutely."[28] But to do so, suggests Kierkegaard, requires passion. As Brueggemann puts it, preachers must be poets who speak a word of vitality against a prose world.[29] It is this word that Martin Luther King, Jr., spoke when he proclaimed, "I have a dream."[30] He spoke with poetry and passion against the prosaic, the unjust, the status quo. Gospel words are words of passion.

Henry C. Gregory tells the story of a young seminary student who returned to his home church and asked permission to recite the Twenty-third Psalm. Permission was granted, and the student stood proudly and recited the entire psalm without a flaw, to applause. Then an old woman stood up in the congregation and hobbled to the front of the church. She also recited the Twenty-third Psalm, but in a weak voice, with poor diction. Yet when she finished, "mothers clasped their children, and fathers who had long been strangers to tears found new fountains."[31] Why the difference? Gregory asks. "The student knew the psalm, but the saint knew the shepherd." The old woman spoke a word of truth because she had lived all the pain and it was reflected in her hunched shoulders and bent back. The student's diction was flawless, but articulation of the word requires more than flawless diction. It requires the ability to speak a truth that comes from the pain of living and that reaches our passion and evokes our tears.

It is this word of poetry and passion that invades and molds the best of preaching. It is no wonder that poetry has so often been used to express the mysteries of love, for love surpasses understanding and poetry is the only language adequate to convey it.

Poetry is a lost art in our world today. Much of what passes for poetry, much even that gets published as poetry, is not genuine poetry but prose that has been broken up into shorter lines, as though the shape alone would render it powerful. If the lines are put back together, they read like prose. Prose is left-brain language, the language of logical connection, of conclusions that follow upon premises, of evidence sufficient to justify judgments made. It is the language of science, of Kantian rationality, of deduction. Prose is a necessary language, and it has a very important place in ethics. When we want to know how the connections are made, how our own living is at the expense of others' dying, prose is the language in which evidence can be lined up in logical fashion so that we may be convinced and even converted. In particular, it can help us make the connections that bring us to conviction and *metanoia*.

At the same time, the power of the Word is not contained in prose. We may be brought to *conviction* by confronting the logical gaps between the evidence and our conclusions, but we will be brought to *grace* by the language of poetry.

To know that we are loved in spite of our faults and failures is not a logical proposition. This is a lived reality, and it must be experienced as a lived reality in order to be believed. The paradox of being loved in spite of our faults—sometimes even because of them—defies logic, but it does not defy the knowledge that faith can bring. There is another way of knowing, the way not of prose and logic but of poetry and pattern recognition.[32] Modern speech tends to be specialized; it tries to achieve precision. The speech of the Bible, by contrast, defies systems and precisions: it is organic and expansive, exhortatory and invitational rather than propositional and precise.[33]

It is this organic, expansive way of speaking that churches need if they are to speak to those dimensions of faith that go deeper than logic. Theology—logos about theos, words about God—is the effort to give expression to faith, which is the reception of God's self-revelation. The revelation comes first, faith is the response, and theology is a third step. Indeed, in liberation theology, it is a fourth step, for one must try to live out one's faith, and theology is the reflection on that effort of living. Faith, the response to God's self-revelation, requires a language appropriate to the immensity of that experience.

As God is beyond all human language, every language is in some sense a betrayal of the power, the mystery, the majesty, the presence of God in our midst. Any image of God is too limiting. Every image of God is too limiting. Even all the images put together are too limiting for the immensity and mystery of God.

This may be why the Bible includes an enormous range of images for God. God is often imaged as mother—mother hen, mother bear, a mother bending over to help a child to walk.[34] God is imaged in both personal and nonpersonal language—in the personal language of "Abba," or "daddy," but also as whirlwind or breath. Exclusive use of male language for God is problematic not just because it is damaging to women or to the human community, but also because it is an inadequate and inappropriate address for God. It is theologically wrong. Indeed, it is idolatry. In spite of the fact that we are warned directly in Scripture against creating "graven images" for God, that is precisely what such language has done: God as Father has become a graven image that violates the commandments. The great "I am that I am" transcends any single image, and all of these images are crucial for expressing God in our midst.

The liberating word, the word of grace, will be a poetic word, an expansive word with the power to break through our everyday expectations,[35] unleash our energies, break down idols, create the balm of Gilead. I go to church to hear this word.

### The Performative Word

Words can have performative power. To say "I promise" is not just to make a statement but to change the nature of the world in which we live. When a couple says "I do," they become a new entity. Two little words create a new reality. They create a new unit in the world—a married couple. They create new obligations, new lines of loyalty and fealty.

So it is for us as a covenant people who live under the promise of God. This promise has performative power. It creates a new entity. It liberates us from the world's ways of doing things, it gives power to weakness, it allows us to believe in a future not dependent upon the past.

Perhaps above all, it is this last that is necessary today. Everyone seems to agree that the golden age in which children could expect to do better than their parents did before them has ended. Studies show that when families live in dead-end circumstances, with no hope for job improvement or advancement, their values change and their children grow up with little hope for the future, little understanding of the importance of delayed gratification, little sense that anything matters except what I can get for me right now. In their monumental study of one segment of American culture, Robert Bellah and his associates called this "instrumental individualism."[36] It is a peculiar form of utilitarian or consequentialist thinking: what is "right" is what gives me satisfaction right now, or what puts me at the top and makes me number one. "Easy credit." "No down payment." "No payments until next year." Such thinking has gained a virtual stranglehold on segments of our society. We live in the fast lane, spending freely, taking whatever we can get, with little thought to the convicting or liberating word.

The gospel message is that the future is not dependent on the past, that this stranglehold can be broken.[37] Human sin and finitude do not have the final word. Even death is not the final word. There is a future not dependent on the evils of the past. There is a future in which the lion and the lamb can lie down together. There is a future in which the horrors of child abuse, the hunger of neglect and social injustice, can be overcome. Even apartheid can be overcome. While we may have to wander in the wilderness for forty years or forty generations or forty lifetimes, there is a promised land.[38]

Sometimes the promise will mean that my expectations must get shattered. Florida Scott-Maxwell writes:

> I often want to say to people, "You have neat, tight expectations of what life ought to give you, but you won't get it. That isn't what life does. Life does not accommodate you, it shatters you. It is meant to, and it couldn't do it better. Every seed destroys its container or else there would be no fruition."[39]

The poetic word, the word of passion, will often shatter our neat, tight expectations. But out of the broken pieces it will grant us glimpses of healing grace. One of the most difficult and painful experiences of my life was going through a divorce that I did not want. All my expectations—even my self-image—were shattered. I never felt like a failure, as so many people assume happens in divorce. But I did feel as though the future had been eroded out from under me, and as though I had lost touch with God. My expectations of the perfect life I would lead certainly came to an end.

But through that experience, I found God in new and joyful ways. The love that friends showered on me, the gentle reminder from a counselor that I might have lost touch with God but God had not necessarily lost touch with me—these experiences brought healing and new life out of the desert of abandonment and despair. Water flowed into the desert, and the heart that lived there became green and verdant.

In the shattering of expectations there may be the experience of death, but there can also be the experience of new life, of joy that overflows. Poetry is the language of joy. It is the language that spills over, breaks boundaries, pierces to the heart. It is a participatory language that not only describes a reality, but also creates one. It invites and invokes. Oppressed people who have found faith are often extraordinarily joyful. In stark contrast to the harsh realities in which they live, they have hope and faith in abundance.[40] It is as though they understand that "the journey is home," as Nelle Morton puts it,[41] or that the cross is the resurrection, as John Howard Yoder might say.[42] Perhaps it is because they have no illusions about this world; it has never been good to them, and they understand full well how it works against their interests. Thus, their struggle for justice brings joy even in the midst of great pain. That struggle is the proleptic living of the reign of God. This is what it means to live the in-between time in life-producing ways.

## Remembrance

### Purposeless Praise

Part of the reason for the joy that spills out even in the midst of pain is that the word spoken and heard is a word of remembrance and anticipation.[43] Oppressed people celebrate in spite of their oppression, because the biblical message is that God has intervened to rescue the slaves in Egypt, to free the prisoners, to lift up the lowly. This memory gives reason for joy.

In order to understand how crucial remembrance is, let me take a little excursus into the interpretation of worship offered by Leander Keck in *The Church Confident*. Keck argues for the "purposeless praise" of God. Indeed, he claims that "unless purposeless praise of God is restored to its central place in worship, mainline Protestantism will not be renewed."[44]

By purposeless praise, Keck means a nonutilitarian approach that is theocentric rather than anthropocentric: our purpose in worshiping is not to build ourselves up, but to acknowledge who God is and what God has done, and to offer thanks to God. Once we introduce into worship a utilitarian concern—for example, using worship to make people "feel" better—then we are trying to manipulate God, and we invert the proper relationship between creator and creature.[45] Praise is just praise, pure and simple, without thought for reward. Praise is focused on the living God, not on ourselves.

Hence, worship must be focused on the living God, not distorted by anthropocentric concerns. While it is true that worship will assist us in getting proper perspective on our lives, being liberated, enlightened, and healed, these are by-products of worship and not the point of worship, argues Keck. Worship is the praise of God. In praising God, we will meet God, and in the meeting with God, history will cease to be as we have imagined it to be.[46]

I find Keck's words both helpful and problematic. It is helpful to be reminded that worship is not, at root, a utilitarian exercise. It is helpful to be reminded that although we are created in God's image, in our modern world we sometimes focus on the image to the point where we lose sight of the original. Following the Human Potential Movement, we are always in danger of replacing the worship of God with the worship of human potential. This is idolatry, and Keck serves us well in offering his caution.

Yet his theocentric focus is also problematic. Faith, and hence worship, is always response to God's self-revelation. But that revelation comes to us through creatures, large and small, through the cosmos, through communities who have struggled to record their experiences of God, through the movement of the Spirit in our midst. Our access to God is always mediated. One cannot "see the face of

God and live." We know God through God's self-revelation, and that self-revelation is mediated by human communities, by the words they have available, and by the world in which those communities are situated. Hence, worship must not be disconnected from the people, or it will be disconnected from God.

## Impassioned Memory

Here, I find Walter Brueggemann helpful.[47] Praise of God that is disconnected from the experience of the people, suggests Brueggemann, runs the risk of becoming abstract and formulaic. "God's love endures forever" can become an empty formula, cut off from specific examples. When this happens, praise of God is rote speech, not impassioned memory. The word has been flattened.

For too many of us who grew up in the church, this is exactly what faith has become—rote speech, not impassioned memory. We say the Lord's Prayer, or the Nicene Creed, or the Beatitudes without connecting them to the concrete history of God's interventions to liberate suffering and oppressed people. "Forgive us our debts, as we forgive our debtors" has been cut off from its link to the jubilee year, from its link to the incredible sense of gift and release that those who have become enslaved economically would feel when told that they will get a fresh start, a new beginning. Cut off from this history, this memory, the words become almost an embarrassment. "What debts?" we want to ask. "I don't have any debts to be forgiven." The concrete memory of what it meant for a people virtually forced into slavery to have their "debts" forgiven is watered down. We lose the power, the mystery, the wonder of what God has done for us. We also lose the challenge to be convicted and to question whether we should not forgive some of the "debts" that are owed to us by other peoples and nations.

When praise is separated from the reasons for praise, it gets toned down and reduced to "barren adjectives and comforting nouns."[48] The reasons for praise are given in the narratives, the stories of what God has done for the people and the stories of what God does for us today. The gospel message is carried not only in the words of the biblical text and in the historical memories of Christian communities throughout the ages, but also in our local churches, small and struggling though they may be. It is crucial that our words keep alive the specific narratives of God's actions in our midst. These are narratives of remembrance and even of "dangerous memory," of subversive tales.

I know of one unlikely church that became a sanctuary for refugees precisely because it kept alive this dangerous memory.[49] The story of the good Samaritan was for this church not simply a pleasant tale about long-ago times. It was a living reality and a story about how God acts in our midst. On the basis of that living reality, a middle-class, middle-America, comfortable, law-abiding church decided that it had to become a sanctuary church, welcoming refugees who entered the United States illegally and sheltering them from the legal consequences. That is not purposeless praise; it is impassioned memory giving rise to ethical behavior.

## God in History

The narratives of Christian tradition affirm that God acts in history. Mainline white, middle-class churches in North America[50] have tended to privatize religion. Although we pray, "Our Father," we focus on our private relationship with God. Jesus did not die for *our* sins, apparently, but for *my* private sins. Lost is a sense that God rules, that God deals with nations,[51] that God judges, that God is on the side of the poor, not necessarily on my side. The worship of a God who acts in history has been replaced by worship of a God who is a Creator outside history, who gets everything started rather nicely and then sits back until it is time to redeem my little individual transgressions. God has been deprived of embodiment in the world, in history, in time and space.

As Brueggemann puts it, uncritical praise of God ends up legitimizing the status quo. Praise must not be separated from the narratives of pain and rescue that name the power of the living God. The living God is not static—not some unmoved mover who pushed a button at the beginning of history and then sat back to wait until it is time to push a button again at the end of history. The living God is active in history. To make this claim is to acknowledge, as Keck suggests, that history as we know it must be reconceptualized. Things that seems like successes may not be. Things that seem like failures may not be. The fact that children will not achieve more than their parents, for instance, is not necessarily a failure of the child or of the system. Things that seem like progress may not be. God's economy is not our economy.[52] The scandal of Christian faith is that the Savior of the world comes to us as a helpless infant and that salvation comes through crucifixion—there is no resurrection without death. This is the understanding of the world that we proclaim in worship.

The Word that we wish to convey with our words is always beyond us. Hence, the words we speak must be multifaceted. For me, to be the word of God they will be words of conviction that connect me to the world around me in ways that enable me to see and claim my obligations. They will be words of passion and poetry. They will be performative words, words of remembrance, words of judgment and grace that have the power to turn the world upside down and shatter my expectations. They will be words that open me up to the mystery that transcends all human categories. The word I need to hear can be a gentle word of invitation or a roaring word of power and praise. And, as we shall see in the next chapter, the Word that convicts, comforts, and calls us is also a nonverbal, embodied word.

# WORSHIP:
# WORD INCARNATE

Several years ago, I was a member of a small congregation that became divided over issues regarding pastoral leadership. It was a difficult time. In spite of our best efforts to reconcile our differences, the church split. Neither side was large enough to be viable by itself, and my worshiping community came to an end. I was plunged into a grief deeper than I could have imagined. I had been a member of the church for five years. The loss of my community, of my communion, was so painful that it was six months before I could set foot in another church; that year, I went through both Christmas and Easter without a church. Remembering the loss still brings tears to my eyes. Such is the power of the worshiping community and of the worship it engenders.

This experience attests to the fact that although Protestants are a people of the Word, words alone do not make a church. Church is a community, a communion of saints. It is the people gathered for worship and for service to the world. In the next chapter I will look specifically at the church in the world. Here, I will focus on worship.

Christians go to church not just to hear the Word preached, but for fellowship, for the rhythm and flow of worship, for the ritual and symbolism and music and prayer and recitation and all the other things that are part of the worship experience with and beyond words. The Word to which we give expression in words is embodied, incarnated, in everything we do. It is given particular embodiment in our worship. If the church is the Body of Christ, then this embodiment is very important. My "exiled" friend who was so happy in her new church loved it not just because the word was well articulated, but because the worship was inclusive and creative. It is not a sermon alone, but an entire experience of worship and of the community formed around that worship that brings people to church.

A young person who is active in the Student Christian Movement writes, "I simply can't see myself attending the pale and limp churches in my town."[1] His imagery depicts a church whose body is fading—it has gone "pale." It is wilting—"limp"—rather than vibrant and strong. If the overall challenge to the churches is posed by the suggestion that we "finish it up," the specific challenge for worship is posed by this imagery of a church that has gone pale and limp. The image suggests a church that is lacking both lifeblood and backbone.[2]

What does it take for churches to have both lifeblood and backbone? What gives embodiment strength? Although I believe that much of the lifeblood and backbone of the church is evidenced in its presence in the world, the gathering of the community for worship is also important. Are there some theological/ethical prerequisites for "good" worship? What must worship be to contribute to the renewal of the church? What must worship be to be the incarnation of the Word? While appropriate worship will differ from place to place and people to people, I think there are some constants that can be discerned for worship if it is not to be limp and pale, but vibrant and strong.

## A Gathered Community

Worship begins with a gathered community, a communion of bedraggled "saints." The Word that we worship is expressed in how we organize ourselves as a community. Two aspects of that gathering seem particularly important to me. They stand in some tension with each other, however, so our approach to them must be carefully nuanced.

First, it is essential that the church be a community rather than just an accumulation of individuals. When I recently moved to a new city, I began looking for a church. The first one I visited was a beautiful old building. But as I sat in the pew and looked around the sanctuary, I noticed something: people sat alone or in couples, but not in groups. They did not greet each other. They did not seem to know one another. Even at coffee hour they remained segregated. They appeared to be a collection of individuals rather than a community. The "body" image that we so often use for the church does suggest that each part can be quite distinct and can function independently of others. It also suggests, however, that the parts are connected and work in harmony. This collaborative function is what makes it a body rather than an assortment of body parts. This sense of community—of "body-ness"—needs to come through in the gathering of the community.

Second, it is essential that the church welcome strangers. One small church that I attended wanted to grow—or so they said. Yet I noticed that when anyone new came to the church, that person was not greeted, not welcomed, not included in coffee-hour conversation. Old-time members were so glad to see each other that they virtually neglected newcomers, who were often left to stand alone feeling awkward and wondering whether they were wanted. In another small church that needed to grow, a newcomer told me that a church member had said to him, "Oh, there's nothing for you to do here; all our committees are full." Where the community is too cohesive, the stranger is not always welcome.

Almost every church I have attended has included with its announcements words of welcome and invitation to strangers. I was particularly pleased by the words of welcome offered during the service of one church I visited recently. So after church, I dutifully signed the guest book and went to the coffee hour. No one spoke to me; no one welcomed me. Being a rather bold person, I introduced myself to an elderly gentleman and asked him to tell me something of the church's history. This he did, at some length. But then he turned away. He asked me no questions about myself or my previous church experience, and he made no effort to introduce me to anyone else. The words of welcome in the announcements were not well "embodied" for me in that church, and I have not returned there. This experience was an important reminder that "only fifteen percent of what we communicate is verbal; the rest—eighty-five percent—comes through non-verbally."[3] If the church wants to be a living embodiment of the Word, it must welcome the stranger.

Yet this is not easy.[4] Indeed, welcoming the stranger stands in direct tension with being a community, because strangers represent a threat to our community in some way. Welcoming the stranger—genuine welcoming of the stranger—does not mean merely allowing the stranger into "our" space. It means that our space will be changed. If we honor the stranger for who she is, and she becomes part of the body, then the body will never be the same again. It has gained a new member, who brings her talents, history, visions, and goals into the fellowship. Genuine welcoming of the stranger requires us to bump up against our cultural or local narrowness, our preconceived ideas of what is acceptable and unacceptable. The church that genuinely welcomes the stranger does not simply let the stranger into a preformed routine, but accepts that the routine itself may be changed. We cannot cling to the past, or to the way things have always been done, because to do so is to deny the validity of the stranger's way of being.

As we become increasingly aware of the plural and multicultural nature of the world in which we live, the challenge of welcoming the stranger while yet remaining community may be the biggest challenge we face. The church that I want to attend will not necessarily know *how* to accomplish this, but it will know that this is the issue and that it must be faced head-on.

### New Structures

Because the church as community is an embodiment of the Word, it is also important for churches to find new and appropriate structures to enable and express that embodiment. The stranger is not welcome so long as structures and practices that exclude some people remain in place. In the previous chapter I spoke of the importance and power of inclusive language. But this is only one of the many changes with which creative churches are struggling.

Another change—and a very difficult one—is the question of leadership style and organizational structure. Although women in ministry remain a minority, they are gaining in numbers in our seminaries. As women take leadership in churches, both in ordained and in lay positions, they may bring a different style to their work.

In *Leading Women*, Carol Becker proposes that women generally do have a distinctive style: they tend to be process oriented rather than goal oriented, to adopt participatory management, to be willing to share information rather than wanting to be the "expert," to stress negotiation and compromise, to have a fundamental concern for relationship, and to be more informal than men have been.[5] This style is not unique to women, but it does challenge some of the hierarchical modes by which churches have traditionally been organized. Having women in leadership positions in the church often makes men—and women—uncomfortable, partly because we are seeing something new, but also because that newness does not fit well our traditional expectations and comfortable assumptions.

Clinging to traditional expectations and comfortable assumptions, however, is what creates a pale and limp church. Churches are full of women, but are women fully welcome there? To welcome them only so long as they do things the "old" way is to treat them as strangers—as powerless outsiders. To say that women are made in the image of God, and then to keep women out of positions of power, or to fail to honor the structural changes that may come from having them in positions of power, is to give a clear message that the stranger is not welcome in our midst.[6] Only by being willing to reconsider our structures and expectations do we genuinely embody the Word in our midst.

This applies to other groups as well. Many churches today remain uncomfortable with openly gay and lesbian members, with members who have disabilities, with people from different cultural and ethnic backgrounds. Where they are desired as members, they may be excluded from leadership positions. This means that the welcome is not yet wholehearted. The community is not yet inclusive, a living embodiment of the Word. Only by being willing to reconsider our structure and expectations do we genuinely embody the Word in our midst.

Because the church community is not yet inclusive, many groups are starting their own congregations. They seek a place where the welcome that embodies the Word is not hypocritical, but thoroughgoing. One of my greatest joys was being genuinely welcomed into a church that had been founded by gay and lesbian people. I had wondered whether straight people would really be welcome there.

To my delight, I found that I was; to my chagrin, I learned that other churches in which I was welcome would not welcome my gay and lesbian colleagues as wholeheartedly as I had been welcomed by them. It was a humbling experience.

Perhaps, above all, genuine welcoming of the stranger requires humility—the recognition that our way is not necessarily right or the only way to do things. I know all too well how difficult this is to do. Many times in my classroom I have struggled to open myself up to new ways of doing things without losing the core of the intellectual tradition that I value highly. But I also know from my own experience how rewarding it can be.

## The Need for Separate Space

Yet, sometimes a church's best efforts to be an inclusive and welcoming community can backfire. Such was the case for a minister friend of mine. An African American family had been attending his new and predominantly white church for some time, and the family was excited about joining the church. But all of a sudden they stopped coming. The minister went to see them to find out why. The father of the family said to him, "Look, no one has been mean or done anything to drive us away. Everyone has been wonderful, but that is just the point. I am concerned that my thirteen-year-old daughter will assume that this is the norm for African Americans in a predominantly white setting. You and I know that it isn't." Although the family's experience had not been bad, the mother and father had decided that their children needed to attend an African American church, where they could learn and worship within their culture and develop the skills needed to deal with the "real" world. They had chosen to drive a considerable distance to church every Sunday in order to provide this key educational and spiritual experience for their children.[7]

This experience struck a deep and painful chord in me. How tragic it is that "the real world" is indeed a world in which racism still runs so deep that we must teach our children to beware of integration. How tragic it is that efforts at integration are fraught with so many perils. Yet perils there are. I want desperately to worship in a church that not only does not exclude anyone, but that makes a conscious effort to include and learn from people with a range of life experiences. Yet when we reach out to those who come from different backgrounds and have different experiences than ours, we run risks.

The first is the risk of assimilation at the cost of identity and history. "Outsiders" can become part of the community so long as they conform to the community and the community does not have to change in order to accommodate them. When this happens, we have learned nothing. There is no *metanoia*, no change, no growth into wholeness. Worse yet, the community might be using outsiders in order to "look good," or to appear politically correct, while nonetheless imposing dominant hegemony.

Another risk is that the community may exploit others for its own purposes. "Teach me what it means to be a Hispanic woman." "Remind us when it is Black History month." "Tell us about sexism." Rather than take responsibility for its own growth and change, the community puts the burden on the one who is seen as "other." I remember vividly the first time a male colleague stood up and protested the use of noninclusive language in worship. I was incredibly grateful for his actions. For the first time, I did not feel that the burden of educating my colleagues fell completely on me. I could be one of the crowd rather than a beacon of whether we were "doing it right." Others could start being the watchdogs of the institution, and I could relax. The burden for change should be shared by *all*, not imposed on the newcomer or left to the responsibility of the stranger to educate the remainder.

For communities that genuinely seek to be inclusive, these are the Scylla and Charybdis of welcoming the stranger: trying to avoid imposing our hegemony, while simultaneously trying to avoid exploiting the other for our benefit. The sad truth is that racial integration has salved many white consciences in America without bringing its promised gifts to black, Hispanic, and Asian communities. There is sometimes a need for separate space for oppressed groups, so their histories and ways of doing things do not get swallowed up by assimilation to the majority. I started my work in ethics because of the ringing words of Martin Luther King, Jr., in "Letter from a Birmingham Jail."[8] I am deeply indebted to King, and I continue to believe in the vision of a truly integrated society. But true integration will involve what Marie Augusta Neal once called "relinquishment."[9] True integration is not simply the perpetuation of the white way. Until we have learned to relinquish power, oppressed groups are correct to be wary of domination and exploitation.

The tasks of the church in gathering as a community are already considerable. In order to embody the Word, the church will need to find its center as a community; it will need to learn how to welcome the stranger without losing its cohesion as a community; it must avoid exploiting those who are "other" while being genuinely ready to learn and grow and to change its structures and ways of doing things accordingly. This is a tall order. And all of this is requisite even as we gather together for worship.

## *The Community at Worship*

When we do gather for worship, what are we doing? I propose that worship is both *praise* and *positioning*. Worship is praise; it is that joyful response to God that issues forth in words of hallelujah in the face of the Creator, Redeemer, and Sustainer. But worship is also positioning; it is the work of the people—liturgy. Worship is an integral part of living a life of response to the Creator, Redeemer, and Sustainer. It positions our lives in relation to God.

Keck contends that "worship enacts and proclaims a construal of reality and of our relation to it."[10] I concur. For me, this construal of reality and positioning of ourselves in relation to it must embody a dialectic of pain and joy, despair and hope, death and resurrection. A church in which tears are never shed is not the Body of Christ. A church in which water is never turned into wine, laughter never raises the roof, and joy never overflows is not the Body of Christ. Failing this embodiment, worship fails to embody the Word. It becomes pale and limp rather than colorful and strong.

Moreover, this dialectic of pain and joy, despair and hope, death and resurrection must connect my pains to the larger groanings of the world. As Hoge and his colleagues suggest in their analysis of baby boomers, I want worship to draw me away from petty concerns so I can remember the larger picture. I want worship to be uplifting and empowering.[11]

But more than that, I want worship to establish a world. Worship does not only proclaim a construal of reality. It enacts that construal. In the very act of praise, in the positioning of our lives in relation to

God, worship makes available to us a different world than the one we normally inhabit. Brueggemann's way of putting it is that the cultic act stands in tension with the workaday world.[12] Precisely because the workaday world is full of oppression and injustice and violence,[13] it is crucial that worship embody an alternative reality.

In our workaday world, we receive hundreds of messages that contradict the reign of God. The workaday world tells us that women's work is not valued—much of it goes unpaid, and what is paid is often paid at considerably less than the comparable work of men.[14] The workaday world tells us that "big boys don't cry"— vulnerability is a liability rather than an asset. The workaday world tells us that people's value comes largely from what they produce or earn—social status depends on income level. The workaday world tells us that unproductive time is "wasted" time—"doing" is more important than "being." The workaday world construes a certain understanding of reality.

Church is where we worship God by enacting and proclaiming a different set of values, a different understanding of reality. At its best, it is where all people—whatever their color, race, sex, politics, income, physical size, personality, sexual orientation, or physical disabilities or differences—are valued, appreciated, respected, loved, helped to perceive and achieve their destiny. It is where we enact a world in which it is what is in the heart, and not what is in the pocketbook, that matters; where caring for children is no less valuable than designing a space shuttle; where giving and receiving love and justice are the core of our way of living and being.

It is because worship is so important for embodying an alternative reality that women today are pushing hard for churches to change their traditional modes of working. The church that vests all power and privilege in the clergy or in those who have always been in positions of power, the church that remains hierarchical and refuses to honor the laity does not embody the reign of God. It simply looks like any other hierarchical organization. The church that neglects women's voices and ignores their gifts does not embody the reign of God. It simply looks like any other sexist organization. The church that makes no effort to extend its boundaries beyond the comfortably homogeneous community is not the reign of God. It simply looks like any other xenophobic institution. Such churches have become pale and limp. They lack the backbone and lifeblood of genuine embodiment.

## Ritual and Rhythm

Clearly, then, worship does not simply remove us from the world. It does not enact a new set of values for a brief period of time—a wonderful moment of respite from the cruelties of a dog-eat-dog world, but separated from the rest of life and really having nothing to do with it. Sunday morning cannot be disconnected from the remainder of the week. Genuine worship will not only enact a new world that must, by its very nature, affect the structures of church, but genuine worship will also place us in creative tension with the structures of the workaday world. The boss who worships on Sunday morning should not be able to go back to unjust work structures on Monday.

Contemporary Western culture has bought into a too-facile separation of public and private spheres. We have come to think of time spent with family as "private" space and of home as a "retreat" from the world. So, too, Sunday worship has all too often become a place of retreat from the world. Like a cave where one can withdraw to lick one's wounds, we come to church to get away from the world with its demands. Church, like family, has been privatized, much to the loss of both. Compartmentalized, sanitized, church becomes little more than an irrelevance, a nice quiet space for those who can afford it or who have nothing more exciting to do on a Sunday morning. (How many churches could compete with the Superbowl?!)

The desire for a retreat from the pains of the world is not altogether wrong. Liturgy—good liturgy—has the power to lift the spirit, to reach to the depths of one's wounded soul and bring the balm of Gilead that makes the wounded whole. I go to church to hear the word of God that convicts. But I also go because I need that ritual, that liturgy that reaches beyond the verbal to the deepest recesses of the soul and offers a binding of wounds for the sake of the struggles yet to come. To be convicted is to be sent out into the struggle. To have our wounds bound is to be sent out into the struggle with strength, with conviction.

This strength, this conviction, comes only through community, through the power of the re-membrance of communion, the power of the binding together that genuine liturgy represents. Whether we are sharing the common cup, passing the peace, or offering intercessory prayers, worship, liturgy, gives us a power to face reality that we would never have on our own. It gives us the power of community. As Kristine Culp puts it, we cannot make our way in the world without communities of faith.[15] People show up on Sunday partly because of an inarticulate yearning for a lost communion.[16] Worship at its best is the expression, articulation, and instantiation of that communion. Liturgy is the work of the people, and good liturgy will always strengthen us for our work in the world. When I lost my communion, my worshiping community, I also lost part of the anchor that keeps me stable in the stormy seas of everyday living.

But this communion is not just a break from the workaday world. It is part and parcel of the wholeness of life lived under God's presence. As Brueggemann puts it, worship creates a world, and the very creation of this world delegitimizes other worlds. It renders them less powerful. The very fact of worship raises a profound challenge to all the values of a sexist, racist, classist, and discriminatory society. The very fact of worship raises a profound challenge to capitalism, socialism, communism, fascism, and all the other "isms" of human life. It may be partly for this reason that the church has often served as a bulwark against racism, sexism, and many other forms of injustice in the world.[17]

Although we think of liturgy as the ritual of the worship service, it is literally the work of the people. There is, then, no separation between liturgy and people's work. Liturgy or worship is praise. And that praise creates a world. The creation of that world is a positioning. The enactment of a different world positions us in life: it positions us for the work ahead, the week ahead, the challenge ahead, the struggle ahead, the hardship ahead. In our in-between lives, worship centers us so that life flows out of its source and toward its destiny.

In *Until Justice and Peace Embrace,* Nicholas Wolterstorff argues strongly for a world-reforming church. Work and efforts to affect social structures are central to Wolterstorff's vision of church. Then he asks, What is the place of worship? Is it merely to get ready or renewed for the struggle?

Wolterstorff's answer is no. Since, in Christian worldview, God is active in the world, the world is sacramental. It is the place where God's grace is manifest. Worship is the response to perceiving the world this way. Both work and worship become responses of gratitude to the grace of God that is manifested in our lives.

Further, Wolterstorff argues that the rhythmic alteration of work and worship is important. Two roots to this rhythmic alteration—to the command to work for six days and hold the seventh as a Sabbath—are found in the Hebrew Scriptures. In Exodus 20:8-11, the Sabbath day is the day on which we rest because God rested on the seventh day after creating the world. In Deuteronomy 5:12-15, the Sabbath day is the day on which we remember and honor God's mighty act of freeing the people from slavery. In both biblical texts, the setting aside of this day is a remembrance of God's mighty acts. It is a remembrance of creation and of liberation. The Sabbath day, the day set aside for worship, is a memorial of remembrance. Just as the Word is a word of remembrance, so the gathering of the community in worship is an act of remembrance.

Therefore, the rhythm of work and worship is important, for it binds all of human life into a memorializing remembrance of *who* we are and *whose* we are. The purpose of worship is not only to strengthen us for the tasks ahead, but to remind us of the *meaning* of those tasks. Worship is preparation for the work ahead, but it is also the proper positioning of that work in our lives. Worship is crucial for giving us proper perspective on work. Without the joy of remembrance, work loses its capacity to remind us of God's presence in our lives and of the sacramental quality of all of life.

## The Sacramental Quality of Life

Traditionally, a sacrament is an outward and visible sign of an inward and spiritual grace. If this is true, then sacraments are not limited in nature or scope. God's grace is not limited to baptism, marriage, Eucharist, death, or ordination, but infuses all of life. All of life, therefore, has the potential to be sacramental. Indeed, all of life should be lived sacramentally—as an outward and visible sign of an inward grace.

William Stringfellow gives expression to this sacramental quality of life in his image of "living Jerusalem in the midst of Babylon."[18] For the Israelites, Jerusalem was the holy city, the symbol of God's shalom in which things would be in right relation. Babylon was the image and incarnation of evil—of oppressive structures, power run amok, injustice reigning. To live Jerusalem in the midst of Babylon, therefore, is to live out of the vision of God's shalom even in the midst of injustice and oppression.

Every encounter between two people is an embodiment of either the presence of God or the presence of evil. Every encounter can enact either Jerusalem or Babylon. Thus, our very words and gestures can be sacraments to one another, ways of embodying God's grace in our midst. Our work, our marriages, our parental responsibilities, and our friendships are all sacramental. All of life has the potential to show forth the grace of God, and this is what Stringfellow boldly proclaims in his image of living Jerusalem in the midst of Babylon.

While all of life has the potential to be sacramental, Protestant churches have traditionally given special recognition to the sacramental character of baptism and Eucharist. In Protestant theology, these are the places where the communion of saints and the grace of God are most clearly made manifest. Perhaps it is appropriate that one of these moments, baptism, is understood to happen only once in a lifetime, while the other, communion or Eucharist, happens on a regular basis. This combination reminds us that God intervenes in our lives both in once-in-a-lifetime occasions and on a regular basis.

At baptism, an individual is taken into the community of the church in explicit recognition of that person's status as a child of God. While mainline churches generally practice infant baptism, the most moving baptism I have ever witnessed was of an adult. Both husband and wife had been attending the church for some time, and they had just had a baby, whom they wished to baptize. However, with some chagrin, the father acknowledged that he had never been baptized; in order to become a member of the church into which his daughter would be baptized, he needed to be baptized. So on the same day, both father and daughter were baptized in the church. Watching a large, strong young man humble himself and ask to be "helped" in faith by the community was one of the most joyful moments I have experienced. While the baptism of infants is an affirmation of the community's commitment to raise these children in a sacramental world, there is a peculiar power in the request of an adult for this sacrament. Baptism, as Donna Schaper reminds us, is about community: "You can't just get sprinkled and leave."[19]

The sacrament of the Lord's Supper is variously called Eucharist or Communion. Each of these terms is helpful in reminding us of the meaning of this special sacrament. Eucharist comes from the Greek term *eucharistias*, or thanksgiving. This term reminds us that our worship is a memorializing remembrance of God's grace. The sacrament is one of the most important places where we enact, remember, and relive the story of what God has done for us. It is for this reason that I prefer the somewhat traditional words of institution: "On the night in which he was betrayed, Jesus took bread and broke it and gave it to his disciples, saying . . ." Words that separate the breaking of bread from the betrayal of Jesus also separate us from our history. Jesus did not simply die, and he did not simply die on a cross. He was betrayed, sold, bargained away, crucified, killed unjustly. The harshness of the story is an important part of understanding the incredible grace that is offered to us through that story. The Eucharist is a thanksgiving of remembrance—a celebration of the memory of God's grace and gifts.

Communion is also a helpful term, because it reminds us that through this common history and remembrance the sacrament binds the people into a community or communion; the sacrament is both a remembering and a re-membering, a bringing together again of the people to be positioned for the struggle ahead.[20] In the sacrament, we find joy in the midst of pain and hope in the midst of despair.

Denominations differ in how often they serve Communion. Some prefer the sacrament to be enacted every time the community gathers for worship, some prefer that it be once a month (often on the first Sunday), and others choose yet a different pattern. While my personal preference is for a frequent pattern, what matters most is not the frequency, but that the sacrament be both a remembering and a re-membering that binds us into a sacramental view of life in which we can discern the signs of the times and see the grace of God in everything.

## The Unity of Worship

Sometimes it is hard to see the grace of God in everything. On the day before I give an exam, my office will be full of anxious students. I may have to grit my teeth and answer the same question twenty-five times—even though I had already answered it in class the day before. On the day after the exam is returned, my office may be full of dismayed students protesting their grades. On such occasions—and at moments almost every day—the grace of God in everything seems distant if not impossible.

I remember one day when I came home late at night, exhausted, having received devastating news that morning and having had no time to deal with it during the day. I thought, "I'll just put my feet up for a few moments and give myself time to grieve and to figure out what I am going to do about this." Wearily I sank onto the sofa, shook off my shoes, and was about to put my feet on the coffee table when I glanced to my left. There, out of the corner of my eye, I could see quite clearly a pool of water forming on the kitchen floor from the pipe that had just cracked under the sink. At times like this, the sacramental quality of life tends to elude me. Is there something in worship that would help me to hold on to my priorities and keep my life focused on God's reign rather than on my sorrows, fatigue, and petty agendas?

Part of what enables me to have a sacramental view of life is worship that knits life into a single unit. If worship is to enact a construal of reality, if it is to embody the faith that moves from despair to hope, from pain to joy, from death to resurrection, then worship must be a unified whole. Each piece must contribute to the enactment, the construal. In good liturgy, the songs, the readings, the sermon, the nonverbal messages—all will be of a piece.

One way to knit life into a unified, sacramental whole is to have worship that builds over a period of time. Advent is the season when we see this most clearly, with the lighting of candles building from one week to the next. But there are ways to achieve this unity and cohesion at other times. Some churches have a set liturgy that provides continuity from week to week. As comforting and enriching as such a liturgy can be, these churches must be careful that the liturgy does not become a rigid form stifling the lifeblood of the church. This is particularly true where laity are not incorporated into that ritual. If liturgy is the work of the people, then let the people do the work! Involving laity in liturgy is central for embodying the construal of reality in which the lowly are lifted up and the world's values are reversed.

Churches that do not have a set liturgy[21] have to work harder at creating unity from week to week. Not enough attention to the form of worship may yield a church that flops too easily from one fad to another and fails to have enough backbone on which to hang its flesh. Lacking backbone, the church will become a limp embodiment. For churches from traditions that lack set liturgies, there are many options to create unity: preaching sermon series, using the same hymn and adding a stanza each week, opening with chants, utilizing visual aids, incorporating dance—many verbal and non-verbal keys can be used to keep the continuity of life over the weeks. This helps to place the stresses of each week within a larger framework that instills meaning into the events of the entire week.

Ironically, one way to achieve a sense of sacramental quality of all life may be precisely to break with the worship traditions with which we are most familiar. The very familiarity may lull us into perpetuating a division between church and world that threatens to leave us with pale and limp embodiment. Some churches have experimented with moving away from the once-a-week Sunday morning worship experience. Some have adopted small cell groups or house churches where clusters of members meet for prayer, fellowship, and worship on a regular basis. Others have moved to a model of several worship services each week—perhaps a more traditional service on Sunday morning, and a service using "new" music and worship forms on Wednesday evening. These models have the advantage of allowing different members to experience worship in the ways that are most meaningful and renewing for those members. Form can be adapted to the particular embodiment that speaks to that portion of the congregation. The specifics of worship are less important than the embodiment of faith.[22]

Whatever the form of the liturgy, the root question is whether it enacts the pain and joy, the death and resurrection, the despair and hope that are the reality of life lived in the gospel. Bland worship avoids both pain and joy. In our anesthetized life, we are so afraid of pain that, in our desire to mute suffering, we sometimes stifle joy.

The gospel is good news. But it is good news in the midst of pain and suffering. There is no resurrection without death. If we try to avoid the pain and suffering, we will also not be able to hear or embody the gospel. We will not incarnate the Word.

The proper balance between form and flexibility will have to be contextualized: embodiment is specific to place and culture. What works in a rural midwestern Lutheran church is not necessarily what works in an urban Baptist church. Each must find a way to be the Body of Christ, the word incarnated living in the in-between times. Each must find a way to balance the needs of continuity with the imperative to welcome the stranger. Each must find structures that are inclusive and creative. Each must find the mode of praise that positions us in the world. It is to that world we now turn.

# WORLD: WORD INCARNATE, AGAIN

T he chapel of Pacific School of Religion, where I have taught for many years, has only one stained-glass window.[1] That window depicts the Great Commission, the sending out of the disciples into all corners of the earth. One does not see the window while worshiping, but only upon leaving the chapel, reminding all who worship there that it is precisely in the going out of church and into the world that we find our deepest communion.

The Word is incarnate not just in worship or in the gathering of the community, but in our presence in the world. Jesus did not preach the church; he preached the coming of God's reign on earth. True word, true worship, does not remove us from life, but positions us within life. We have abandoned the social gospel conviction that we can simply establish God's reign on earth, but the biblical vision remains a compelling call to do what we can toward establishing freedom, justice, equity, and shalom. "If you love me, you will keep my commandments" (John 14:15). Those who are called into covenant with God are called into service to others in the interests of God's reign. This means that we are not called *out* of the world, but *into* it.

So, I go to church not only to hear the word or to join the communion of bedraggled saints in worship, but because the world is full of pain, injustice, alienation, hunger, misery. Church is not an escape from this pain and hunger and misery, but a place in which there is a promise that transcends the pain of human life. It is the place where we are reminded that we are not alone in the struggle, that God suffers with us, that there is life strong enough to transcend even death. I go to church not to be separated from the world, but to be reminded of the sacramental quality of life, to be positioned within the struggle for justice, to be given the strength with which to make the world a better place. Church brings us back to the word of God, with all of its convicting force; it offers the strength of community that enables us to sustain that conviction and be hopeful in the midst of pain; and it sends us forth into the world imbued with conviction, strength, and joy to face the struggles that lie ahead. This chapter is about that sending forth.

## On Living Jerusalem in the Midst of Babylon

A firm conviction of Protestant theology is the "priesthood of all believers." Each of us has a ministry. We perform this ministry in the world—within our families, jobs, communities. They become extensions of the Body of Christ. Church is not a building. It is not a worship service. It is not a one-hour-a-week phenomenon. Church is a people who understand their identity to be formed by allegiance to a story, and who commit their lives to the meaning of that story. The church is the community that announces good news to the world.

That announcement must be embodied, lived, incorporated into the very structures and ways of being in the world. As the Body of Christ, the church is called to enact the good news. In Stringfellow's phrase, we "live Jerusalem in the midst of Babylon."[2] The world around us lives in chaos, chained to disvalues of mammon, competition, and domination. This is Babylon. In Protestant tradition in particular, we understand ourselves as living under the Fall. Different denominations and churches will perceive the meaning of this metaphor differently, but for all Christians, the Fall at least symbolizes the sin, disorder, and distortion in which we seem consistently to live. The Fall affects all of creation: We contend with powers and principalities, not just with individual sins. We live under the power of death.

Resurrection has to do with breaking the power of death. This is what it means to live Jerusalem in the midst of Babylon. The church lives a Jerusalem vision, a vision based on a different set of values, a different understanding of the meaning of history. Jerusalem, for the ancient Israelites and early Christians, was the holy city, the "city of the living God" (Heb. 12:22). Jerusalem stands for all that God desires and promises in the midst of a broken and unjust world.

We are called to sacramental living—to finding the grace of God in the mundane events of everyday life, to seeing how our small actions are symbolic of larger universes of meaning, to doing justice, loving mercy, and walking humbly with our God. One of the most moving experiences I have had in church happened during a series of Sundays in which laypeople took turns talking about how they try to embody faith in their workaday worlds—how laying tile, or running a shelter for abused women, or doing graphics as an independent businessman could be a way of trying to live out the meaning of Christian conviction. This series of witness stories was a powerful reminder that church and world are not separated, and that our deepest communion comes in the effort to embody the Word in all that we do.

## A Covenant People

For many, if not most of us, this effort to live out the gospel message in our daily life will be the best we can do as individuals. We can, as Donna Schaper challenges us, invite the poor to *our* table, not just to a local service center.[3] The contemporary phrase is "practice random acts of kindness." This captures at least a part of what it means to live Jerusalem in the midst of Babylon, for it grasps the sense that small acts can be symbolic of larger universes of meaning, and that every act of justice, love, or humility counts. But lest we think that living Jerusalem in the midst of Babylon is a simple matter of being kind to our neighbor, let us take another look at what it means to be a covenant people. Practicing random acts of kindness captures part, but only part, of what it means to live Jerusalem in the midst of Babylon.[4]

We are a covenant people. Because we depend on God's covenant, our future is not bound by our past. God breaks into our lives, cuts across our expectations, offers new beginnings. This is what liberation theologians mean when they talk about utopia. Utopia is not some perfect world, for we know that we live within the Fall. Our world will never be perfect. But it is possible to envision a future that is unfettered by the mistakes and injustices of the past. Whether we call this forgiveness or jubilee, it is God's promise to us that the future is never simply an extension of the past. It is possible to envision a future in which "right relationship" reigns, in which justice is the norm, in which the lion and lamb lie down together. In a world torn by violence and war, in a world where the gap between rich and poor grows continually, there is little evidence that the lion could ever lie down with the lamb. But we know that this is God's will, and we live in the vision of what that promise means.

To live in this vision is not simply to offer small acts of kindness, as important as those are. Nor is it merely to attempt to live our everyday lives ethically, adhering to moral standards of fairness, truth telling, and the like. Rather, it requires that we *judge* our present history for its failure to live up to the reign of God.[5] Our world always stands under the judgment of the Realm to which we are called and which is promised to us. As Ed Farley puts it, the gospel means we bring Jesus to bear on the present so that it is both judged and drawn in hope toward redemption.[6] Jesus is the prolepsis of the kingdom, the prefiguring of the reign of God. We are given a glimpse *in* history of the meaning *of* history. To affirm that Jesus is Christ is to affirm that all of history is henceforth understood in light of this prefiguring.

Ethics, therefore, cannot be a simple matter of my little sins or of random acts of kindness, as important as they are.[7] I felt compelled to help Mary and Tom when I found Mary shivering in the cold that Advent season. Nothing substitutes for that direct hands-on intervention. Yet such interventions do nothing to change the basic system within which Mary and Tom are caught. If the church is to embody good news in the world, it must find ways to live that do not allow destructive systems to continue. Ethics has to do not merely with individual acts or character, but with the entire shape of the age. William Coats suggests that to reduce ethics to slogans such as "obeying the law of love" is to assume that this age is generally healthy and needs only to be reformed; it is to ignore the deep wounds that indicate the power of death in our lives. If death holds sway over us, then faith seeks a breaking of death's power in the world. Only radical change—change that goes to the roots—will accomplish this. Only a power sufficient to stand up to the power of death can break our bondage to Babylon.[8]

How, then, does one live out the meaning of affirming that Christ is Lord—that God reigns, that we are called into a covenant in which a future of right relationship is promised? I want to suggest three modes of action, which correspond to classical notions of the pastoral, prophetic, and priestly tasks of ministry.

## *Presence*

If we begin with the reality of human suffering, then one mode of affirming that Christ is Lord in the world is "suffering with" the other, or compassion. Compassion is often expressed through presence, sometimes called accompaniment. Presence has been urged by feminists and liberation theologians alike.[9] It implies being present with the poor and oppressed, with those who suffer, living their lives, accepting their burdens, coming to understand. "Until you have walked a mile in my shoes, you don't know me" might be the slogan of a ministry of presence.

Presence is real, tangible: it means sharing the danger, the horror, the disease, the limitations of someone's life. Presence is also powerful, symbolic: someone loves me enough to be here beside me, to share my burdens, to hope for my future, to covenant with me toward that future. Presence accepts vulnerability and finds strength in it. In a review of David Hilfiker's reflections on being a doctor with the poor, Arthur Frank is moved to suggest that "the quality of helplessness that can come only from being there, not as a visitor but as one sharing the ground of suffering, seems prerequisite to moral reflection."[10] Not as a visitor, but as one sharing the ground of suffering—this is the hard work of presence. It may be prerequisite to understanding and, therefore, a necessary precursor to any ethical action. Accompaniment accepts its powerlessness, but in that very acceptance it can become the ground for more adequate seeing and, therefore, for more adequate acting.

In a world oriented toward contract, presence and accompaniment can be a powerful enactment of covenant. Increasingly, Western nations seem to act out of a sense that we will do only what is good for us. We take a contract approach to life: I'll do something for you only if you do something for me. (Another version of this may be: I'll do something only if I get the satisfaction of knowing that I can change things the way I want.) Contracts are limited, specific. They provide for an exchange: I do this, but in return I get that.

By contrast, Christians understand ourselves to be bound in covenants of life with life. We do not simply stick it out until something better comes along. We are covenanted. We take the bad with the good, we "hang in there," we struggle together. A covenant is neither limited (God's *hesed* endures forever) nor specified (you do this and I'll do that). A covenant binds life with life, history with history, community with community.[11] In a world taken over by contract, the church witnesses to a different way of understanding our presence with each other. We are to be covenanted with all God's people, everywhere, not just with those of our own nationality. Presence is a *pastoral* task to which the priesthood of all believers is called.

## Liberation

But a ministry of presence is only a beginning. If presence is the pastoral task to which we are all called, then liberation is the *prophetic* task to which we all are also called.

The world groans under the burden of oppression. Everywhere there is poverty, disease, illiteracy, and struggle for survival. Mothers in Brazil triage their own babies, allowing some to die in order to give others a chance to survive.[12] In the face of such stark realities, it is not merely presence that is needed, but liberation. To be with those who suffer but not be moved to end that suffering is to fail in compassion. Compassion suffers with the other, but it also moves to end the suffering.[13] This movement is liberation.

Liberation theology has perhaps pushed us farther than any other theology toward understanding that one cannot worship God without simultaneously working to make the world a better place. Theologies of struggle, theologies of *han*,[14] theologies of pain—the voices of oppressed people around the world call out to all the churches to embody Christ by liberating the oppressed, setting the captive free, bringing sight to the blind.

Liberation has two movements: the movement of denunciation and the movement of annunciation. The first task is to perceive clearly where and why oppression is happening and to denounce the structures, systems, and ideologies that support it. This is the first prophetic political task. If "misery is not innocent,"[15] then it is the task of a world-formative church to try to understand the causes of that misery. Here, liberation theologians, apocalyptic ethicists, feminists, and some North American theologians are all in accord that the world must be seen as a single system or "empire." Because the world works as a single system, there will be no liberation for the oppressed that does not require relinquishment on the part of those who are privileged. The oppressions must be denounced, even if that makes the privileged uncomfortable.

The second prophetic political task is the annunciation of an alternative—of a world of justice and shalom, of liberation and peace. There is joy—not just in River City, but in the church— because the establishment of right relationship means that all God's people will be truly free. While the naming of what is wrong is the first step toward liberation, liberation is not complete without the envisioning of an alternative, a "utopia" in the sense of a future not confined to the errors and sins of the past.[16] Both are part of the prophetic task to which the Body of Christ living in the in-between times is called.

## *Reconstruction*

When basic liberation has been gained—when apartheid is overturned, when walls of political repression crash down in Eastern Europe—then there is a need for reconstruction. If accompaniment is the pastoral task, and liberation the prophetic task, then reconstruction may be the *priestly* task of the political church. This task involves bringing about order and keeping the structures of justice going, as well as recognizing what in our traditions and histories needs to be preserved even in the midst of radical change and hope for new beginnings.

Denouncing the current system and announcing a new system are difficult enough. But even harder is to figure out how we move from the vision and hope for liberation to the actualities of difficult social policies designed to make our world more fair and more livable. Even if we agree that women and members of minority communities have been oppressed and must be liberated, for example, we will not necessarily agree on the mechanisms to achieve an equitable future. Few issues have been more divisive than those surrounding affirmative action or preferential treatment for women and members of minority groups. We know that something must be done to counteract the long history that has resulted in imbalanced power and economic status among groups of people, but we also know that everything we do in order to accomplish this will create some new injustice.[17] The church needs to turn serious attention to these matters of reconstruction.

In a united Germany, for example, Christians will struggle over how to resolve land disputes between the descendants of Jews who lost their land in the days just prior to the Second World War, and the descendants of non-Jews who have now lived on that land for several generations and for whom it may be their only home. In South Africa, too, there will be difficulties over resolving how to apportion lands between black and white occupants whose claims are based on conflicting histories. Reconstruction takes political astuteness to determine which policies will serve the rebuilding of communities, nations, and peoples. Reconstruction also takes a willingness to live with some of those policies and the new injustices they appear to create, for the sake of the common good.

## On the Ethical Ecclesia in the Midst of Diversity

But here we have a difficulty: How can we know what is in the interests of the common good? As firmly as I believe in a world-reforming Christianity,[18] so also must I firmly acknowledge the difficulties associated with such a view. We live increasingly in a world in which we are aware of our differences, and in which we try to affirm those. Pluralism, diversity, multiculturalism—whatever catchword we use, these words point to a fundamental problem for a church that would live Jerusalem in the midst of Babylon. How can we know what "Jerusalem" is? Can we impose our values and judgments on others? In a pluralistic world, are the days of shared ethical values long past? Is there any place at all for the denunciation of what is and the annunciation of good news?

Recognition of pluralism creates serious problems, both for the field of Christian ethics and for the church. On the one hand, we recognize differences in values between cultures, and we want to honor those cultures. We also recognize that much of what we think and perceive is the result of our own social location, and that those who come from different social locations will and should see things differently. Thus, we do not wish to impose value judgments on those whose histories and cultures have brought them to a way of seeing and of being in the world that is different from ours. This is a movement of respect for the otherness of the other. Such respect is required by justice, and it is good.

At the same time, does recognition of cultural differences mean that we then lose any common ground from which ethical judgments can be made? Do justice and respect mean allowing any and all practices that are indigenous to other cultures? Should female circumcision be tolerated out of respect for other cultures? What about genocide? When does respect for differences dissolve into ethical relativism and an inability to challenge the world at all? When does respect for differences disintegrate into a failure to care?

David Hollenbach suggests that we have come to a "crisis of faith."[19] We have lost any assurance that we can make normative judgments about what constitutes a genuinely good society. We are afraid that any assertion that "this is good" will be merely a reflection of our own self-interests. We have become suspicious toward all traditions, ideologies, and theories. We are rightly cautious of repeating historical mistakes. Christian triumphalism has a sad history of arrogance and of efforts to impose our views and values on others. Such efforts are rightly to be decried. But in that process, we must not forget that to be a Christian is to affirm something about the meaning of history. Unless we announce and attempt to live out that meaning, we are not being true to our faith. What, then, can we do?

There are difficult theoretical issues to be resolved here. Discussions of possible grounds for a common morality currently permeate the field of Christian ethics. Some have tried to reinstate a modified view of natural law, in which those virtues necessary for the common good might be recognized across cultures.[20] Others have proposed that in the very demands of conversation, there are grounds for basic rules that work across cultures: our very ability to be in dialogue with those who are different from us already presupposes some common morality.[21] Some have argued for a modified Kantian view of a common structure to rationality that might provide grounds for universal judgments about right and wrong.[22] Many have turned to "human rights" language to find ground for judgment about practices in different cultures.

Others, of course, stress the distinctiveness of Christian ethics and reject the notion of a universal morality in which Christians would share moral norms with other traditions.[23] Hollenbach proposes that the distinctiveness of the cross can, in fact, become a window onto something that is universal. In the cross we have a God who suffers with all of suffering humanity. The cross therefore opens the possibility of an ethic of "compassionate solidarity." The pursuit of universality in ethics, suggests Hollenbach, "means that the reality of human suffering wherever it occurs must be central in the quest for some form of common morality."

I take my beginning where Hollenbach does: in the reality of suffering in the world.[24] How should the church respond to this suffering?

## On Letting the Church Be the Church

One answer to this question is offered by John Howard Yoder from his Mennonite tradition, and by Stanley Hauerwas, representing mainline (Methodist) church tradition.[25] "Let the church be the church" both argue. By this they mean that the task of the church is to witness to a different way of living, not to try to reform the world. The world can be largely ignored, as the church becomes an alternative to it. Hauerwas argues that the church is called to become a certain kind of community, and that it is within that community that the witness to God is made manifest. The church witnesses to the world not by trying to change the world, but by showing that it is possible to live by a different set of values and virtues.

This image draws me. First, I agree wholeheartedly that the church should not identify with any particular state or political formation. It distresses me to find American flags in churches in the United States. The church is the Body of Christ and is for all God's people. It is genuinely international, and I therefore believe that it should avoid signs and symbols that identify it with particular nationalities or political agendas.

Second, this image draws me because of the difficulty and necessity of attending to the internal structures of the church. It is difficult enough to deal with the moat in one's own eye without trying also to attend to the speck in another's. If we are called to embody the Word, then where better to begin than with one's own house?[26] I have always believed that one should try to get one's own house in order before criticizing one's neighbor. Changing the church is hard enough to do, and would probably take a lifetime, without ever getting around to trying to change the world.

Third, "let the church be the church" draws me because it suggests a division between church and world, and there are many places where I think the church should stand over against the world. For instance, the secular world is generally organized hierarchically. The church can provide an alternative model by being organized laterally or collegially.

Fourth, among the strengths of this vision—at least, as articulated by Stanley Hauerwas—is the focus that it puts on welcoming the stranger. The church is called to be a certain kind of community—a community that lives in trust, that welcomes the stranger. Drawing on the biblical injunction to welcome the sojourner in the land, Hauerwas suggests that the church must become a community of people who offer hospitality to the stranger.[27] There is evidence that, historically, the church has done precisely this on many occasions. The church is often the one place where those who are mentally retarded are genuinely welcomed as full members of a community. The church was sometimes—though, sadly, not always—on the forefront of the struggle for racial justice. "Strangers" have been welcomed into a community of believers who live out a vision different from the dominant vision in the world around them.

For all these reasons, the image of letting the church "be the church" and letting the world "be the world" is somewhat compelling. The church might simply offer to the world the witness of a community that lives with a different set of values, virtues, and organization. This would be "living Jerusalem in the midst of Babylon" without trying to reform Babylon.[28]

## Sect vs. Church: On Being Self-consciously Political

Nonetheless, there are some problems with the vision of "letting the church be the church" as it is interpreted by Yoder and Hauerwas.

First, is the church simply to ignore the world, or is it to attempt to witness to the world by being an alternative? If the church is to be an alternative community, then one must determine, "alternative to what?" Is the church to resist every societal move, or only some? If chastity becomes the new norm among secular young people, surely the church would not encompass sexual licentiousness just to be different! Here, no doubt, both Yoder and Hauerwas would say that the church does not derive its standards from the world, either by way of affirmation or by way of rejection. The church's standards come out of its own history and faithful response to God's self-revelation.

But that raises yet another problem: how to interpret that history and response. Hauerwas places hospitality to the stranger at the core of the church's mission and vision. This is his interpretation of the core message of the biblical faith. By way of contrast, I note that the injunction to offer hospitality to the stranger can only be understood in the larger context of the history of liberation of the people from Egypt. It is because the Israelites were strangers and sojourners in the land that they are now enjoined to offer hospitality to the stranger. So the place of hospitality is dependent upon the history of liberation. The story that gives rise to the norm of hospitality is a story about the liberation of the people.

I would argue, therefore, that liberation is the more fundamental theme, and that the church ignores its own history if it fails to embody liberation. But there is no way to embody liberation without being politically active. Simply offering shelter or opening doors of hospitality will not bring about liberation. People can be "helped" and yet still kept in their place. Liberation, according to biblical understanding, always involves liberation from concrete political, social, and economic threats.[29] Thus the church that focuses on being an alternative community, rather than liberating those who are oppressed by the political and economic structures of society, has forgotten its own history and the meaning of that history.[30]

Finally, it is virtually impossible to be "in, but not of" the world. Short of withdrawing into communities as separated from the world as are the Amish, for example, it is not possible to exist in society without being affected by it.[31] How many churches have renounced their tax-exempt status? If they have not, then they benefit from the structures of society, and they cannot claim simply to be apart from that society. The assumption that the church can retreat from the world[32] assumes a kind of division of spheres akin to the division between public and private spheres. It does not work.

The church that would attend to the realities of the lives of its members, therefore, has no choice but to be political. The question is not whether it will be political, but what kind of political presence it will take. A different vision of church from "let the church be the church" is offered in Calvinist history. The great American theologian Reinhold Niebuhr argued that the church is world-transforming: it is meant to be involved, it is political. In fact, our very presence in the world is a political statement.[33] Jesus did not simply die, and he did not simply die on a cross; he was crucified. Here at the center of our faith is a paradigmatic political image of state justice gone awry.[34] The church that is founded on that story cannot help making a political statement—a statement about power, and justice, and about the right ruling of the world.

## *Finding Norms for the Struggle*

But what should be the content of that political statement? As the church faces the world during a time of pluralism, it is difficult to know what norms might indeed be universal, or what approach to ethics can both honor Christian tradition and recognize the need for cross-cultural standards. I propose two modest standards as a beginning toward a common morality.

The first I draw from Donald Shriver's recent study, *An Ethic for Enemies: Forgiveness in Politics.*[35] Shriver argues (pace Reinhold Niebuhr!) that justice alone is not sufficient for political relations. Indeed, he proposes that forgiveness is both historically demonstrable and ethically necessary for our common life on this earth.

Through a fascinating historical study of three examples—black-white relations in the United States, German-U.S. relations following World War II, and Japanese-U.S. relations following the same war—Shriver shows how time and time again, those who might be considered enemies found it both politically astute and morally necessary to seek and to offer forgiveness. They acknowledged wrongdoing, acted to forgo vengeance, exercised empathy for the enemy, and sought renewal of relationship.

This is a cross-cultural vision, historically and politically rooted, that supports the most fundamental of Christian affirmations: the role of repentance and forgiveness in God's grace. Shriver's discussion suggests that even in a very divided world—a world at war, a world permeated with racial injustice—there is hope for a common morality that works toward renewal and right relationship. If Shriver is correct, then Christians can both seek and urge forgiveness as a universal standard that not only reflects Christian tradition, but that concurs with the best in international politics.[36]

The second modest standard I draw from Roger Hutchinson's proposal for "sustainable communities."[37] Hutchinson proposes that in a culturally diverse society, Christians cannot take for granted the primacy of Christianity, but Christians can still affirm that Jesus came so that we might have fullness of life. "In a pluralistic society the aim of a Christian program, or a Christian piety and politics, will be to create a society in which others may come to the fullness of life consistent with shared public standards and with the teachings of different traditions." Since there can be no fullness of life without sustainable communities, Hutchinson proposes that sustainable communities provide a minimal standard within such a pluralistic vision.

I concur with Hutchinson's vision. Yet, I also wish to push it further. If fullness of life is the goal, then communities must be not only sustainable, but full: they must allow not simply for survival, but for shalom. This is the vision to which we are drawn by an incarnational theology: God came so that we could have life and have it abundantly. The Word is among us working for justice, love, and peace in the world. Sustainable communities would be a minimal standard. Even to achieve this, those of us who are wealthy by world standards must be ready to let go of our privileges. But the ultimate goal is not merely survival; it is for all to have fullness of life. No child on the Alto de Cruzeiro in Brazil should have to be triaged so that other children can survive. No child in America should be homeless and hungry on the streets. The standard must provide not simply for sustainable communities, but for sustenance without triage and death. It must provide not simply for sustenance, but for nurture, care, and growth into fullness.

We will never overcome all the pain and suffering and injustice in the world. Only God can do that. But the fact that our efforts will not eliminate suffering does not mean that they are worthless. If we do not make the effort, we will fall into despair. If we make the effort expecting it to succeed, we will fall into despair. Our hope lies not in our efforts, but in God. Yet precisely because it lies there, we are called into compassionate solidarity through pastoral, prophetic, and priestly roles in the world. We can be guided by forgiveness and aimed toward the vision of fullness of life. It is for this that the Word was made flesh and dwelt among us.

The renewal of the church, therefore, requires attention to the world. It is there in the suffering, the pain, the hurt, the alienation, that the church offers a gospel message of hope, joy, meaning, peace, renewal, justice, and love. When the world is renewed—when forgiveness is practiced and communities are not only sustainable but abundant—then the church will also be renewed.

# CONTRADICTION

W hen asked what the opposite of an Introduction was, Winnie the Pooh didn't know, but Owl chimed in and declared it was a Contradiction.[1] So this is a contradiction. An in-between life often feels as though it is full of contradictions, so perhaps Owl was a wise old bird, after all!

The chapters of this volume have explored four Ws of Christian living: word, worship, world, and wonder. As Christians, we stand in wonder before the divine, we long for the word that convicts and comforts, and we worship in order to praise God and to position ourselves for living in the world. While these four Ws would probably be shared by all Christians, the specific articulation given to them here is undoubtedly biased and blinded by my social location and limited vision. After a colleague criticized my initial articulation severely, I hesitated to complete this task, fearful that I would simply be engaging in hegemonic discourse—pretending to speak in dialogue with others, but in reality imposing my own views or seeming oblivious to others.[2] I am keenly aware that my voice is only one that is needed in this dialogue, and I hope this little volume will stand as an invitation to others to join in discourse. I offer these thoughts tentatively, secure in the knowledge that where I am wrong my colleagues will not hesitate to correct me.

Of one thing I am absolutely sure: God makes all things new. That includes the church. That includes my ruminations. That includes life at every level from microbiology to political systems. Whether the renewal of the church is important or necessary may not be in our hands. The Spirit moves in mysterious ways and has the power to create the reign of God in spite of us. Before the mystery of God, we can but walk humbly, hope to do justice and love mercy, and retain a sense of the wonder of it all.

# NOTES

## In-Between Living

1. Douglas John Hall, *The Future of the Church: Where Are We Headed?* (The United Church Publishing House, 1989), p. v. Hall does not agree with this view, but reports that it seems to be increasingly prevalent.

2. Joseph Sittler, *The Anguish of Preaching* (Philadelphia: Fortress Press, 1966), p. 54.

3. In *Common Sense About Men and Women in the Ministry* (Washington, D.C.: The Alban Institute, 1990), Donna Schaper suggests that significant renewal of the church "would require a fast exit" from existing frameworks, "a crucifixion if you will," p. 54.

4. Dietrich Bonhoeffer, *Life Together*, trans. John W. Doberstein (San Francisco: Harper, 1954), p. 18.

## Wonder

1. In *Confessions of a Knife* (New York: Simon and Schuster, 1979), p. 85, Richard Selzer describes his first entry into a church at age twelve; he was overcome by the stained glass, the high ceilings, the statuary and saints, the candles, the smell of incense.

2. In *The Lion in Winter*, there is a scene in which King Henry asks Eleanor for a "little peace." She replies: "Only a little? Why so modest? Why not eternal peace—now there's a thought!" So perhaps we should not ask for only a "little" wonder, but we should beware what we are asking if we ask for more!

3. *Random House College Dictionary*, rev. ed. (New York: Random House, 1975), s.v. "wonder."

4. Oliver Sacks, *An Anthropologist on Mars: Seven Paradoxical Tales*, (New York: Alfred A. Knopf, 1995), p. 287.

5. Peck says that he made this point in *The Road Less Traveled;* he reiterates it in *Further Along the Road Less Traveled: The Unending Journey Toward Spiritual Growth* (New York: Simon and Schuster, 1993), p. 81.

6. Richard Selzer, *Mortal Lessons: Notes on the Art of Surgery* (New York: Simon and Schuster, 1976), p. 46.

7. Oliver Sacks, too, writes of his awe at the capacity of patients to transcend their limits: "Against all odds, Miss H. has always managed to be a real person and to face reality without denial or madness. She draws on a strength unfathomable to me, a health which is deeper than the depth of her illness." See *Awakenings* (New York: HarperCollins, 1990), p. 140.

8. Joseph Sittler, *Gravity and Grace: Reflections and Provocations*, ed. Linda-Marie Delloff (Minneapolis: Augsburg Publishing House, 1986), p. 16.

9. Helmut Thielicke suggests that humans can be viewed in two ways: in their usefulness for us, or in their own being as a child of God. Helmut Thielicke, "The Doctor as Judge of Who Shall Live and Who Shall Die," *Who Shall Live? Medicine, Technology, Ethics*, ed. Kenneth Vaux (Philadelphia: Fortress Press, 1970). Wonder sees—or rather, beholds—the other as a child of God.

10. Selzer, *Mortal Lessons*, pp. 27-29.

11. Karen Lebacqz, *Professional Ethics: Power and Paradox* (Nashville: Abingdon Press, 1985), chap. 7.

12. See the Preface to Larry Dossey, M.D., *Healing Words: The Power of Prayer and the Practice of Medicine* (San Francisco: Harper San Francisco, 1993).

13. In fact, Dossey proposes that we have entered a "third era." The first was that of physicalist medicine; the second that of the mind-body connection; and the third is that of nonlocal medicine, which recognizes the power of prayer to affect people at a distance. See Dossey, *Healing Words*, pp. 39-44.

14. Ibid., pp. 45-53 and passim. Drawing on such studies, there now is a clever advertisement showing one twin drinking a cold drink while the twin three thousand miles away experiences the relief of thirst!

15. I experienced this firsthand some years ago. I had been diagnosed with a cancerous condition in my cervix, but had told no one, quietly scheduling the necessary surgery. I was giving a public lecture and someone from the audience came up to me and said, "Your body is green and healthy everywhere except in your mid-section; there, something is wrong."

16. Dossey, *Healing Words*, p. 111. This research has been replicated elsewhere.

17. Ibid.

18. For example, the subjects trying to influence the random event generator at Princeton could do their praying/thinking before the generator was turned on, and it appeared to be influenced; they could also do their praying/thinking after the generator had completed a run, and it appeared also to be affected. See Dossey, *Healing Words*, pp. 113-21.

19. The notion of interconnectedness or fundamental relationality is also a core claim of modern feminism. In contrast with the autonomous, independent self so lauded in Western, male-dominated Kantian rationality and ethics, feminists have argued for a profoundly interconnected, relational understanding of self and for care and empathy as basic categories of ethical being in the world. It seems that this alternative way of thinking is now being vindicated as mainline thinkers extend their horizons of knowledge in light of new scientific data. See Carol Gilligan, *In a Different Voice* (Cambridge, Mass.: Harvard University Press, 1982); Nel Noddings, *Caring: A Feminine Approach to Ethics and Moral Education* (Berkeley: University of California Press, 1984); Mary Belenky et al., *Women's Ways of Knowing: The Development of Self, Voice, and Mind* (New York: Basic Books, 1986). Of course, there are also critiques of the relational self and of caring as the primary ethical stance.

See Mary Jeanne Larrabee, ed., *An Ethic of Care: Feminist and Interdisciplinary Perspectives* (New York: Routledge, 1993).

20. M. Scott Peck, *Further Along the Road Less Traveled*, p. 76.
21. Ibid., p. 77.
22. Dossey, *Healing Words*, p. 35.
23. Ibid., p. 15.
24. Peck, *Further Along*, p. 78.
25. Ibid., p. 79.
26. Joseph Sittler, *Essays on Nature and Grace* (Philadelphia: Fortress, 1972), pp. 89-90.
27. The Human Genome Project is a $3 billion, fifteen-year international project that hopes to identify precisely the makeup and location of all the genes of the human body.
28. Evelyn Fox Keller, *A Feeling for the Organism: The Life and Work of Barbara McClintock* (New York: W. H. Freeman and Co., 1983), p. 168.
29. Ibid., p. 170.
30. Ibid., p. 148.
31. Madeleine L'Engle, *A Wrinkle in Time* (New York: Farrar, Straus, & Giroux, 1962). The story about the writing of this book has always been inspiring to me. L'Engle took it to publisher after publisher who rejected it. More than ten years went by, during which L'Engle wrote because she felt compelled to follow her creative outlet, but she was not successful at getting her material published. Finally, more than a decade after it was written, *A Wrinkle in Time* was published, and it won the 1963 Newberg Medal Book Award.
32. Kosuke Koyama, *Three Mile an Hour God: Biblical Reflections* (Maryknoll, N.Y.: Orbis Press, 1980).
33. Keller, *A Feeling for the Organism*, p. 148.
34. Catherine de Hueck Doherty, *Not Without Parables: Stories of Yesterday, Today, and Eternity* (Notre Dame, Ind.: Ave Maria Press, 1977), p. 103.
35. Koyama, *Three Mile an Hour God*, p. 27.
36. Friedrich Nietzsche once said, "One skill is needed . . . for the practice of reading as an art: the skill to ruminate, which cows possess but modern man lacks." *The Genealogy of Morals* (New York: Doubleday, 1956), p. 157.
37. Oliver Sacks, *Seeing Voices: A Journey Into the World of the Deaf* (New York: HarperCollins, 1990).
38. Ibid., pp. 75-98, 111.
39. Ibid., p. 141. Dr. Katherine Black of Claremont School of Theology specializes in the use of sign in worship. When she was at the Graduate Theological Union, I often had the privilege of watching her graceful movements as she signed sermons and lectures.
40. Ibid., p. 162.
41. Norman Cousins, *Anatomy of an Illness* (New York: W. W. Norton, 1979).
42. Deepak Chopra, trained in Western medicine, has now become very well known for his efforts to combine Ayurvedic medicine with Western healing. See his *Ageless Body, Timeless Mind* (New York: Harmony Books, 1993).
43. The other major reason was respect for the elderly. Christians are perceived as being kindly and respectful to the elderly, and this drew Chinese, who have a long tradition of such respect, to churches.
44. See Linda J. Clark, *Music in the Churches* (Washington, D.C.: The Alban Institute, 1994).

45. Ibid., p. 5.

46. Fortunately, we are beginning to have some excellent new materials available, such as *Sound the Bamboo* (Quezon City, Philippines: R. R. Yan Printing Press, 1990), which collects hymns from a variety of Asian contexts, and *Voices United* from the United Church of Canada.

47. Montreal *Gazette*, 13 April 1995, p. B2.

48. In a recent video on the generation gap, a young woman says, "Who understands us? Our music does." Morris Massey, *Just Get It*.

49. As L. William Countryman reminds us in his remarkable book *Dirt, Greed and Sex* (Philadelphia: Fortress Press, 1988), Jesus did not believe that we are made dirty or clean by what goes *into* our mouths but by what comes *out* of them! See Mark 7:15-23 and Countryman's discussion on pp. 84-86.

50. In the film *Choosing the Light*, a woman indicates that the bread and wine have been desecrated for her since her experiences of sexual abuse at the hands of her pastor. There is nothing sacrosanct in bread and wine per se. This film was produced by the Milwaukee Synod of the Lutheran Church in America.

51. Kneeling is still used in Anglican Communion services, and it is still used for reception of the Eucharist in some Protestant churches, but in many churches we simply sit through the entire service, receiving bread and wine at our seats.

52. In the times I witnessed such devotion at the Oratoire, I never saw a Caucasian person make the long, slow climb. Is it possible that it is only those who are marginalized who still appreciate the ways in which pain is an avenue to the divine?

53. Kosuke Koyama, *Pilgrim or Tourist: 50 Short Meditations* (Singapore: Stanford College Press, 1974), pp. 1-3.

## *Word*

1. There are a few exceptions—e.g., Quakers, or Friends, who come from the counter-Reformation tradition.

2. Although I have used the language of "hearing," this is not to imply that worship must be filled with sound. As we have seen in chapter 1, silence has a crucial role to play, and "listening to the silences" may be our most profound worship experience.

3. Here, I differ from Keck, who begins with worship, and roots his analysis in the centrality of praise. See Leander E. Keck, *The Church Confident* (Nashville: Abingdon Press, 1993). Although I, too, see the praise of God as definitive, praise is a response to the revelation of God. For a people of the book, that revelation is often first known through the Word.

4. Dean R. Hoge, Benton Johnson, and Donald A. Luidens, *Vanishing Boundaries: The Religion of Mainline Protestant Baby Boomers* (Louisville: Westminster/John Knox, 1994), pp. 204-5.

5. Ibid.

6. Indeed, I suspect that desire for this inspiration and guidance lies behind parental concerns for religious education: parents want their children to form the values that will allow them to sustain a sense of their worth and place in the world when confronted with racism, prejudice, the deeply misogynist messages of much contemporary rock music, or the temptations of drugs and easy escapes.

7. The first two parts of my definition can be found in *Merriam Webster's New Collegiate Dictionary*, 9th ed., s.vv. "convict" and "conviction," respectively.

8. The names have been changed, but the story is true.

9. Indeed, the great theologian Helmut Thielicke argued against social welfare programs precisely because he saw them as undermining the genuine respect for the other required by agape. While I disagree with Thielicke on the question of social welfare, I agree with him on the necessity for agape to offer genuine relationship and respect for the other. See Karen Lebacqz "Alien Dignity: The Legacy of Helmut Thielicke for Bioethics," in *Religion and Medical Ethics: Looking Back, Looking Forward*, ed. Allen Verhey (Grand Rapids, Mich: Eerdmans, 1996).

10. See Karen Lebacqz, *Justice in an Unjust World* (Minneapolis: Augsburg, 1987).

11. This study was done by the Nashville *Tennessean* and reported in the Louisville *Courier-Journal*, September 30, 1995, p. A12.

12. Quoted in Charles Avila, *Ownership: Early Christian Teaching* (Maryknoll, N.Y.: Orbis Books, 1983), p. 50.

13. Ibid., p. 77.

14. Beverly Wildung Harrison, *Making the Connections: Essays in Feminist Social Ethics*, ed. Carol S. Robb (Boston: Beacon Press, 1985).

15. Richard Preston, *The Hot Zone* (New York: Anchor Books, Doubleday, 1994), p. 383.

16. For a full exposition of the ways in which women's work is systemically disadvantaged, see Carol S. Robb, *Equal Value: An Ethical Approach to Economics and Sex* (Boston: Beacon Press, 1995); also Pamela K. Brubaker, *Women Don't Count: The Challenge of Women's Poverty to Christian Ethics* (Atlanta: Scholars Press, 1994).

17. To say that it can happen this way is not to say that it always does. There is a right-brain element in conversion as well, because a genuine conversion results in new forms of pattern recognition.

18. Technically, in the field of ethics, this distinction between blame and responsibility can be seen as a distinction between the subjective and objective realms of morality. Blame is assessed as personal fault; it is deeply subjective. Responsibility, however, does not imply that I am at fault, but only that there are structural realities that must be assessed. While the distinction between objective and subjective dimensions can be overdrawn, this is one place where it is helpful. We can be responsible, objectively speaking, without in any way being blameworthy, subjectively speaking.

19. Yoder suggests that perhaps it was never practiced. See John Howard Yoder, *The Politics of Jesus* (Grand Rapids, Mich.: Eerdmans, 1972), p. 69.

20. I would also argue that there is need for regret, which is not the same as guilt. When we hear of a friend's misfortune and we respond instinctively, "Oh, I'm so sorry," we are not presuming that we are guilty, but only expressing our regret at the misfortune.

21. In my first book, *Professional Ethics: Power and Paradox* (Nashville: Abingdon Press, 1984), I proposed that one of the crucial roles of the pastor is the framing of language with which ethical issues are addressed. Here I am suggesting that this is the role of both pastor and church.

22. Roberta C. Bondi, *Memories of God: Theological Reflections on a Life* (Nashville: Abingdon Press, 1995), p. 27.

23. Ibid., p. 47.

24. See Marie Marshall Fortune, *Sexual Violence: The Unmentionable Sin* (New York: Pilgrim Press, 1983).

25. Patricia Reilly, "The Religious Wounding of Women," *Creation Spirituality*, Spring 1995, excerpted from *A God Who Looks Like Me* (Ballantine, 1995).

26. See Reilly, *A God Who Looks Like Me*; see also Elizabeth Johnson, *She Who Is* (New York: Crossroad, 1994), ch. 3.

27. Judith Mullins, "Birth and Rebirths," in *Women Pastors*, ed. The Birkshire Clergywomen and Allison Stokes (New York: Crossroad, 1995), p. 67.

28. Søren Kierkegaard, *Fear and Trembling*, trans. Alastair Hannay (New York: Penguin Books, 1985), p. 70.

29. Walter Brueggemann, *Finally Comes the Poet: Daring Speech for Proclamation* (Minneapolis: Fortress Press, 1989), p. 3.

30. The text of this famous speech is available in James M. Washington, ed., *A Testament of Hope: The Essential Writings and Speeches of Martin Luther King, Jr.* (San Francisco: Harper San Francisco, 1986), pp. 217-20.

31. Henry C. Gregory III, "The Shepherd," in *Outstanding Black Sermons*, ed. J. Alfred Smith (Valley Forge, Penn.: Judson Press, 1976), p. 39.

32. Those who are familiar with the striking research done on left-brain and right-brain activities (more accurately: the left and right lobes of the brain) will recognize logic as the domain of the left lobe and pattern recognition as the domain of the right.

33. Joseph Sittler, *The Structure of Christian Ethics* (Baton Rouge: Louisiana State University Press, 1958), p. 5.

34. Paul R. Smith, *Is It Okay to Call God "Mother"? Considering the Feminine Face of God* (Peabody, Mass.: Hendrickson Publishers, 1993).

35. What could be more unexpected than to propose that God comes to us not on wings of power or chariots of fire but with all the fragility of a newborn child or a rose in winter? And yet this is precisely the way the Christian faith understands God's surprising presence in our midst.

36. Robert Bellah et al., *Habits of the Heart* (Berkeley: University of California Press, 1985).

37. Ted Peters, *Futures: Human and Divine* (Atlanta: John Knox Press, 1978).

38. Of course, we must never forget that the promised land is full of giants!

39. Florida Scott-Maxwell, *The Measure of My Days* (New York: Penguin Books, 1968). Florida Scott-Maxwell was a Jungian analyst; these reflections were written when she was in her eighties.

40. Lebacqz, *Justice in an Unjust World*; see also Mev Puleo, *The Struggle Is One: Voices and Visions of Liberation* (Albany: SUNY Press, 1994) for a picture of the joy that people living in abject poverty can feel.

41. Nelle Morton, *The Journey Is Home* (Boston: Beacon Press, 1985). This is a classic in feminist theology.

42. John Howard Yoder, *The Politics of Jesus* (Grand Rapids, Mich.: Eerdmans, 1972).

43. Sittler called it a "rhetoric of recollection," a way of "testifying forward by recollecting backward." Joseph Sittler, *Essays on Nature and Grace* (Philadelphia: Fortress Press, 1972), p. 31.

44. Keck, *The Church Confident* (Nashville: Abingdon Press, 1993), p. 38.

45. Ibid., p. 35.

46. Ibid., p. 33.

47. Brueggemann, *Israel's Praise: Doxology Against Idolatry and Ideology* (Philadelphia: Fortress Press, 1988).

48. Ibid., p. 104.

49. Nelle G. Slater, ed., *Tensions Between Citizenship and Discipleship: A Case Study* (New York: The Pilgrim Press, 1989).

50. For a view of the Canadian situation, see Roger Hutchinson, "Piety and Politics: A Protestant Perspective," *Westminster Affairs*, vol. 7, no. 2 (Summer/Fall 1994), p. 11. (A publication of The Westminster Institute for Ethics and Human Values; this issue presents the plenary addresses to the conference on "Ethics and Spirituality: Forging Links" on 4 November 1994.)

51. William Coats, *God in Public: Political Theology Beyond Niebuhr* (Grand Rapids, Mich.: Eerdmans, 1974).

52. This is what Catholics call "discerning the signs of the times." It also reminds me of Letty Russell's notion of "calculated inefficiency." See Letty M. Russell, *The Future of Partnership* (Philadelphia: Westminster Press, 1979), p. 74.

## *Worship: Word Incarnate*

1. Bruce Gilbert, "The Sinking Ship," *Raging in the Streets: Redefining Ministry for the 21st Century* (London: SCM Press, 1994).

2. Certainly, it is not the first time that such charges have been made, especially against white middle-class churches. Some years ago, Mongameli Mabona, reflecting from a black African perspective, lamented that he found Christian worship stilted and restrained. "Let there be less cringing and scraping in liturgy," Mabona implored. Mongameli Mabona, "Black People and White Worship," *Black Theology: The South African Voice,* ed. Basil Moore (London: C. Hurst & Co., 1973), p. 107.

3. Roy M. Oswald, *Clergy Self-Care: Finding a Balance for Effective Ministry* (Washington, D.C.: The Alban Institute, 1991), p. 3.

4. Indeed, this is a place where I would criticize Stanley Hauerwas, who stresses hospitality to the stranger without much apparent recognition of the complexities therein. See Stanley Hauerwas, *A Community of Character: Toward a Constructive Christian Social Ethic* (Notre Dame: University of Notre Dame Press, 1981).

5. Carol E. Becker, *Leading Women: How Church Women Can Avoid Leadership Traps and Negotiate the Gender Maze* (Nashville: Abingdon Press, 1996), pp. 38-41.

6. Ada María Isasi Díaz gives poignant expression to the link between being made in the image of God and being excluded. She talks of a time when she was not accepted for final vows in the convent and she reflects: "This experience of rejection made me think that there was no God, because in moments of rejection like that one I feel I am no good. And if I am no good, how can there be any God? Am I not made in the image and likeness of God?" In Katie G. Cannon et al. (The Mudflower Collective) *God's Fierce Whimsy: Christian Feminism and Theological Education* (New York: The Pilgrim Press, 1985), p. 106.

7. Communication from Roy P. White, 9 January 1996.

8. The text of this historical address can be found in James M. Washington, ed., *A Testament of Hope: The Essential Writings and Speeches of Martin Luther King, Jr.* (San Francisco: Harper San Francisco, 1986).

9. Marie Augusta Neal, *A Socio-Theology of Letting Go: The Role of a First World Church Facing Third World Peoples* (New York: Paulist Press, 1977).

10. Leander E. Keck, *The Church Confident* (Nashville: Abingdon Press, 1993), p. 25.

11. Dean R. Hoge, Benton Johnson, and Donald A. Luidens, *Vanishing Boundaries: The Religion of Mainline Protestant Baby Boomers* (Louisville: Westminster/John Knox, 1994), p. 205.

12. Walter Brueggemann, *Israel's Praise: Doxology Against Idolatry and Ideology* (Philadelphia: Fortress Press, 1988), p. x.

13. See Karen Lebacqz, *Justice in an Unjust World: Foundations for a Christian Approach to Justice* (Minneapolis: Augsburg, 1987), chap. 1.

14. See Pamela Brubaker, *Women Don't Count: The Challenge of Women's Poverty to Christian Ethics* (Atlanta: Scholar's Press, 1994); also Carol S. Robb, *Equal Value: An Ethical Approach to Economics and Sex* (Boston: Beacon Press, 1995).

15. Kristine A. Culp, "The Nature of Christian Community" in Rita Nakashima Brock et al., *Setting the Table: Women in Theological Conversation* (St. Louis: Chalice Press, 1995).

16. Walter Brueggemann, *Finally Comes the Poet: Daring Speech for Proclamation* (Minneapolis: Fortress, 1989), p. 43.

17. It is, of course, sadly true that the church has not always been a bulwark against injustice. See Lebacqz, *Justice in an Unjust World*, chap. 2.

18. William Stringfellow, *An Ethic for Christians and Other Aliens in a Strange Land* (Waco, Tex.: Word Books, 1973).

19. Donna Schaper, *Common Sense About Men and Women in the Ministry* (Washington, D.C.: The Alban Institute, 1990), p. 61.

20. See Lebacqz, *Justice in an Unjust World*, for further discussion of remembrance and re-membering.

21. These are sometimes called nonliturgical churches, but this term is inaccurate. These churches also have liturgy, but the liturgy is nonregimented. It is partly for this reason that I have sometimes used the terms "worship" and "liturgy" interchangeably. Technically, liturgy refers to certain rites or rituals that are part of worship; but worship is also defined as practice with its creed and ritual, and hence overlaps with liturgy. (*Webster's New Collegiate Dictionary* 1974, s.vv. "liturgy" and "worship").

22. My own faith tradition and roots are closely related to my desire both for structure and for flexibility. The United Church of Christ was formed of the union of four church groups who committed themselves to becoming one church in Christ. Their vision of one church under Christ was so strong that each group gave up aspects of worship that had been particularly central and meaningful to them in order to unite into one church. Particular forms were cast off as necessary to move toward their vision. If they erred, it was in the direction of flexibility, giving up form as needed to unite with one another. Coming out of this tradition, I tend to favor churches that are flexible rather than rigid in form and function.

## *World: Word Incarnate, Again*

1. Pacific School of Religion is an interdenominational Protestant seminary and is one of the schools of the Graduate Theological Union in Berkeley, California.

2. William Stringfellow, *An Ethic for Christians and Other Aliens in a Strange Land* (Waco, Tex.: Word Books, 1973).

3. Donna Schaper, *Common Sense About Men and Women in the Ministry* (Washington, D.C.: The Alban Institute, 1990), p. 25.

4. Barry Stenger, "Deliberate Kindness," in *Ethics and Policy*, Spring 1995 (a publication of the Center for Ethics and Social Policy, Graduate Theological Union, Berkeley, Calif.).

5. William Coats, *God in Public: Political Theology Beyond Niebuhr* (Grand Rapids, Mich.: Eerdmans, 1994).

6. Edward Farley, "Preaching the Bible and Preaching the Gospel," *Theology Today*, vol. 51, no. 1 (April 1994), p. 101.

7. Barry Stenger, "Deliberate Kindness," *Ethics and Policy*, Spring 1995, cautions that the slogan "practice random acts of kindness" threatens to deflect our attention away from the structural causes of poverty. I concur.

8. Historically, this is what was meant by saying that Jesus is Lord of History. It means that the entire shape of history comes under the judgment of God.

9. Brita Gill, "A Ministry of Presence," in *Women Ministers*, ed. Judith L. Weidman (San Francisco: Harper & Row, 1981).

10. Arthur W. Frank, "An Agenda for Professional Reflection: Place, Power, and the Other of Medicine," *Second Opinion 21*, no. 1, July 1995, p. 54. This review covers several volumes, among them David Hilfiker, *Not All of Us Are Saints: A Doctor's Journey with the Poor* (New York: Hill and Wang, 1994).

11. William F. May, *The Physician's Covenant: Image of the Healer in Medical Ethics* (Philadelphia: Westminster Press, 1983).

12. Nancy Scheper-Hughes, *Death Without Weeping: The Violence of Everyday Life in Brazil* (Berkeley: University of California Press, 1992).

13. See, for example, Matthew Fox, *A Spirituality Named Compassion: And the Healing of the Global Village, Humpty Dumpty, and Us* (Minneapolis: Winston Press, 1979), pp. 1-8.

14. *Han* is a Korean term that has to do with the deep resentments built up by a history of oppression of the people. See Chung Hyun Kyung, *Struggle to Be the Sun Again: Introducing Asian Women's Theology* (Maryknoll, N.Y.: Orbis Books, 1990), p. 23.

15. Leonardo and Clodovis Boff, *Salvation and Liberation: In Search of a Balance Between Faith and Politics* (Maryknoll, N.Y.: Orbis Books, 1985), p. 4.

16. Liberation theologians are sometimes denounced for being "utopian." But in fact they do not hold out the possibility of creating a perfect world, but only the possibility of creating a world not bounded by past sins.

17. For the great American theologian Reinhold Niebuhr this was a constant theme. See D. B. Robertson, ed., *Love and Justice: Selections from the Shorter Writings of Reinhold Niebuhr* (Gloucester, Mass.: Peter Smith, 1976), pp. 46-51; cf. Lebacqz, *Justice in an Unjust World*.

18. Nicholas Wolterstorff suggests that being "world-reforming" is characteristic of Calvinist faith. See *Until Justice and Peace Embrace* (Grand Rapids, Mich.: Eerdmans, 1983), chap. 1.

19. David Hollenbach, "Social Ethics Under the Sign of the Cross," *Annual of the Society of Christian Ethics*, 1996, p. 3.

20. Jean Porter, *The Recovery of Virtue: The Relevance of Aquinas for Christian Ethics* (Louisville: Westminster/John Knox, 1990).

21. Seyla Benhabib, *Situating the Self: Gender, Community, and Postmodernism in Contemporary Ethics* (New York: Routledge, 1992).

22. Gene Outka and John P. Reeder, eds., *Prospects for a Common Morality* (Princeton, N.J.: Princeton University Press, 1993).

23. Hauerwas tends strongly in this direction.

24. See Lebacqz, *Justice in an Unjust World*.

25. John Howard Yoder, *The Politics of Jesus* (Grand Rapids, Mich.: Eerdmans, 1972); Stanley Hauerwas, *A Community of Character* (Notre Dame: University of Notre Dame Press, 1981), chap. 4.

26. When I was a graduate student many years ago, a number of students and faculty at Harvard worked at the center for Population Studies. This center was a pioneer in studying the results of the world's population explosion. It was here that I first learned what later became commonplace: that in terms of use of the world's energy supply and resources, each child born in the United States uses up proportionately far more of the world's resources than does a child born in India or Africa. Yet we often think that it is India and Africa that have the "population problem." Colleagues working at that center often had large families of their own, and continued to bear children in spite of their academic study of the impact of such practices. This kind of splitting off of one's own life decisions from one's knowledge about the world never made any sense to me.

27. Hauerwas goes so far as to argue that welcoming the stranger precludes abortion, for the fetus is a stranger in our midst. See *A Community of Character*, chap. 12.

28. This is, in fact, what Stringfellow seems to suggest, for he proposes that we "not strive to undo the power of death, knowing that death is already undone." *An Ethic for Christians and Others in an Alien Land*, p. 152.

29. See Gustavo Gutierrez, *A Theology of Liberation* (Maryknoll, N.Y.: Orbis Books, 1973). This is the classic text in liberation theology.

30. Of course, the converse is also true: people can be "liberated" or given rights, but without hospitality those rights can be an empty shell. As Richard Steele put it in his poignant reflections on being the father of a daughter with severe disabilities, it is not the "stairs" but the "stares" that ultimately discourage him and his daughter. They thus need not only access, but welcome. Richard B. Steele, "Accessibility or Hospitality? Reflections and Experiences of a Father and Theologian," *Journal of Religion in Disability and Rehabilitation*, vol. 1, no. 1, 1994, pp. 11-26.

31. The Amish come the closest to achieving this total separation; in a sense, they are not really "in" the world at all, since they make every effort to have nothing at all to do with the rest of the world.

32. For example, Adolf von Harnack once described the "limits within which the church must confine its activity" to be such that it had "nothing to do with . . . practical questions of social-economics. . . ." Quoted in José Miguez Bonino, *Toward a Christian Political Ethics* (Philadelphia: Fortress Press, 1983), p. 26. Harnack's assumption clearly is that it is possible for the church to confine itself to "spiritual" matters that have nothing to do with practical problems of poverty and the like.

33. Cf. Roger Hutchinson, "Piety and Politics: A Protestant Perspective," *Westminster Affairs*, vol. 7. no. 2, Summer/Fall 1994 (a publication of the Westminster Institute for Ethics and Human Values, London, Ontario), p. 10: "In contrast to sects and cults, the 'great tradition' of the United Church [of Canada] was characterized by a church-type sense of responsibility for the social order."

34. Jesus' birth is also depicted in political terms: there was a census, and an effort to kill all male children, because his presence was considered a threat. This political story accounts for Jesus being born in a stable while his parents were in transit.

35. Donald W. Shriver, *An Ethic for Enemies: Forgiveness in Politics* (New York: Oxford University Press, 1995).

36. To say that forgiveness in the public arena is possible is not to say that it is easy, however. In 1969, when the Black Economic Development Council sought reparations from Jewish synagogues and churches who acknowledged their

complicity in an unjust system, almost none sought forgiveness or offered reparations. See Robert S. Lecky and H. Elliot Wright, *Black Manifesto: Religion, Racism, and Reparations* (New York: Sheed and Ward, 1969).

37. Roger Hutchinson, "Piety and Politics: A Protestant Perspective," *Westminster Affairs,* vol. 7, no. 2, Summer/Fall 1994, p. 11.

## *Contradiction*

1. A. A. Milne, *The House at Pooh Corner* (New York: E. P. Dutton, 1961), p. ix.

2. A sharp criticism of hegemonic discourse is offered in Katie G. Cannon and Carter Hayward, "Can We Be Different but Not Alienated?" in *Feminist Theological Ethics: A Reader,* ed. Lois K. Daly (Louisville: Westminster/John Knox Press, 1994).